Country Artwalks from Maine to Maryland

Marina Harrison and Lucy D. Rosenfeld

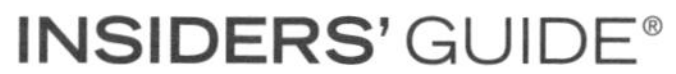

GUILFORD, CONNECTICUT

AN IMPRINT OF THE GLOBE PEQUOT PRESS

INSIDERS' GUIDE®

Text design by Lisa Reneson
Map by Lisa Reneson © Morris Book Publishing, LLC

Library of Congress Cataloging-in-Publication Data
Harrison, Marina, 1939-
Country artwalks from Maine to Maryland / Marina Harrison and Lucy D. Rosenfeld. — 1st ed.
p. cm.
Includes index.
ISBN-13: 978-0-7627-3665-2
ISBN-10: 0-7627-3665-8
1. Art, American—Northeastern States—19th century. 2. Art, American—Northeastern States—20th century. 3. Artists' studios—Northeastern States. 4. Gardens—Northeastern States. 5. Northeastern States—Tours. I. Rosenfeld, Lucy D., 1939- II. Title.
N6513.H375 2007
709.74—dc22

2006036050

Manufactured in the United States of America
First Globe Pequot Edition/First Printing

Contents

Preface ix

How to Use This Book xi

In the Artists' Footsteps: Painters' Views of the World around Them 1

1. Landscape and History on the Hudson Highlands
West Point, New York 3

2. Samuel Colman's Vision of Storm King Mountain
Cold Spring, New York 9

3. Modernists in the Adirondacks
Lake George, New York 12

4. Fitz Hugh Lane, Luminist of the Northeast Seacoast
Gloucester, Massachusetts 16

5. The Hudson River Painters at Kaaterskill Falls
Kaaterskill, New York 20

6. Starrucca Viaduct: Progress amid Natural Beauty
Susquehanna Valley, Pennsylvania 28

7. Offshore Art Colonies
Appledore, Deer, and Monhegan Islands, Maine 31

8. Grandma Moses in Rural New York
Eagle Bridge, New York 39

9. Cape Cod's Mecca for Artists
Provincetown and Truro, Massachusetts 44

10. William Sidney Mount, Long Island's Genre Painter
Setauket, New York 50

Works in Process: Studios, Workshops, and a Glass Factory 55

11. Wheaton Village: Historic Glassworks
Millville, New Jersey 57

12. Folk Art and Modern Craft Workshops at Peters Valley
Layton, New Jersey 61

13. A Crafts Village in the Catskills
Sugar Loaf, New York 66

Artistic Landscapes: Formalizing Nature 69

14. Old Westbury Gardens: Elegance on Long Island
Old Westbury, New York 71

15. Monument to the Coal Miners
Frostburg, Maryland 74

16. Ladew Topiary Gardens: Plant Sculpture in Eccentric Forms
Monkton, Maryland 77

17. Wethersfield: The Delights of Trompe L'Oeil
Amenia, New York 80

18. Opus 40: A Bluestone Environment
Woodstock, New York 84

19. Untermyer Park: The Neoclassical Tradition
Yonkers, New York 87

20. Innisfree Garden: Bringing Chinese
Landscape Painting to Life
Millbrook, New York 91

21. Cedaridge Farm: Impressionist Paintings Brought to Life
Pipersville, Pennsylvania 95

22. Madoo: An Abstract Expressionist Painter's Garden
Sagaponak, New York 99

23. Green Animals: A Topiary Kingdom Made of Yew
Portsmouth, Rhode Island 102

24. A Lower Hudson River Valley Art Tour
Hastings-on-Hudson to Beacon, New York 105

Master Painters and Sculptors of the Past: Artists' Homes and Ateliers 111

25. An Impressionists' Boardinghouse
Old Lyme, Connecticut 113

26. Chesterwood: The Home and Studio of Daniel Chester French
Stockbridge, Massachusetts 122

27. The Thomas Cole House and Frederick Church's Olana
Catskill and Hudson, New York 128

28. Aspet: Home and Studio of Augustus Saint-Gaudens
Cornish, New Hampshire 133

29. Weir Farm: Home and Studio of J. Alden Weir
Ridgefield, Connecticut 142

30. Locust Grove: Home, Studio, and Grounds of Samuel F. B. Morse
Poughkeepsie, New York 148

31. East Hampton's Artistic Heritage and the Pollock-Krasner House and Study Center
East Hampton, New York 151

Outdoor Collections: Art in Public Settings 157

32. Pyramids, Gothic Arches, and Classical Temples at West Laurel Hill Cemetery
Bala-Cynwyd, Pennsylvania 159

33. Masterworks on Campus at Princeton University
Princeton, New Jersey 172

34. Queens' Left Bank: The Noguchi Museum and Socrates Sculpture Park
Long Island City, New York 180

35. Snug Harbor: Contemporary Art and a Chinese Scholar's Garden
Staten Island, New York 187

36. De Cordova Sculpture Park: Modern Forms upon a Hill
Lincoln, Massachusetts 193

37. An Inviting Sculpture Park on Corporate Grounds: The Donald M. Kendall Sculpture Gardens at PepsiCo
Purchase, New York 198

38. Griffis Sculpture Park: Contemporary Works in a Natural Setting
Ashford Hollow, New York 206

39. Two Historic Cemeteries in New York City: Artistic Monuments and Artists' Graves
Green-Wood Cemetery, Brooklyn, New York, and Woodlawn Cemetery, Bronx, New York 209

40. Spectacular Sculpture and Scenery at Storm King Art Center
Mountainville, New York 223

41. Grounds for Sculpture: Fairgrounds Turned Art Site
Hamilton, New Jersey 229

42. José Clemente Orozco: A Master's Murals at Dartmouth College
Hanover, New Hampshire 231

Choosing an Outing 235

Index of Artists, Architects, and Selected Art Sites 238

About the Authors 244

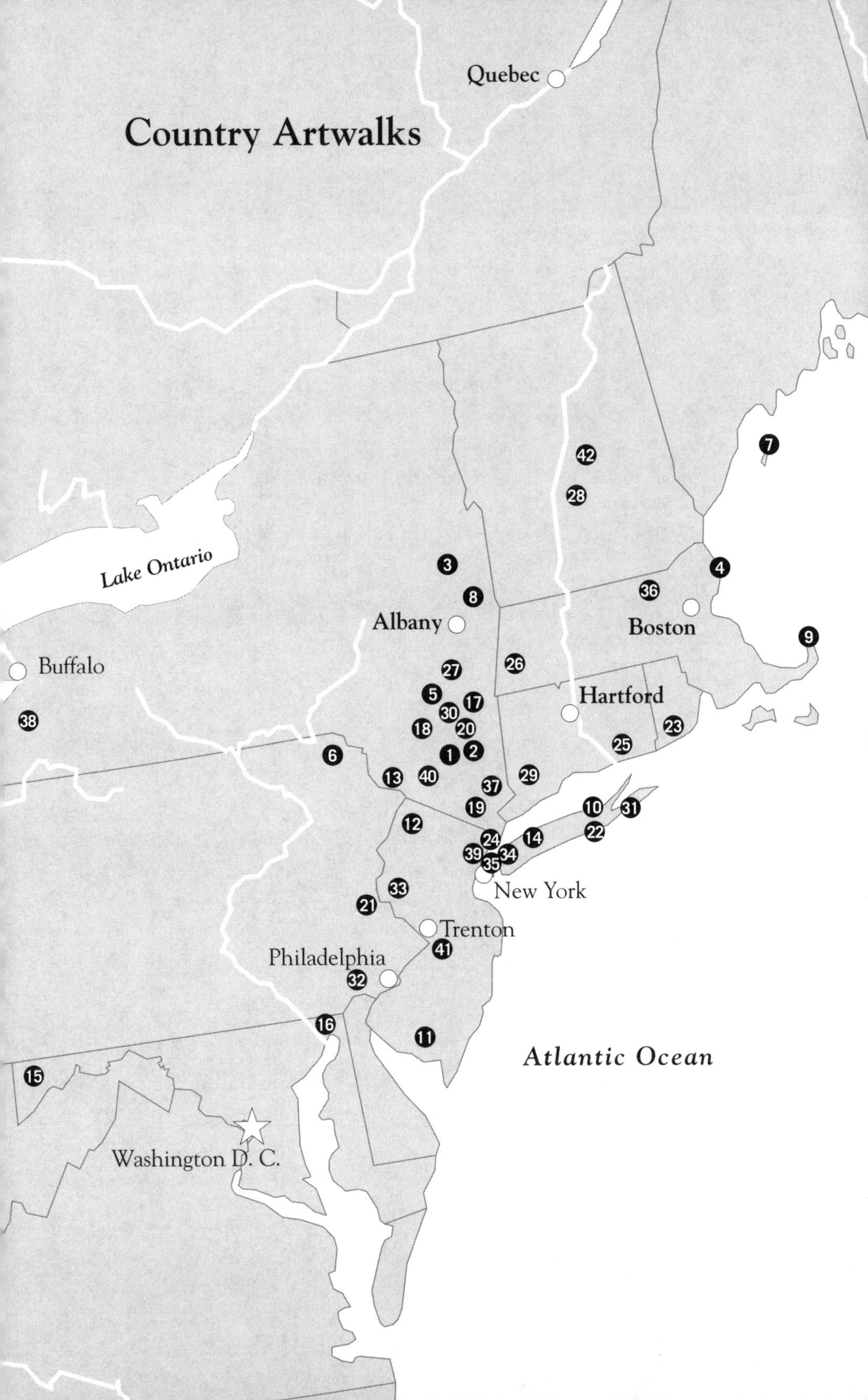

Country Artwalks
Quebec
Lake Ontario
Albany
Buffalo
Boston
Hartford
New York
Trenton
Philadelphia
Washington D. C.
Atlantic Ocean
1
2
3
4
5
6
7
8
9
10
11
12
13
14
15
16
17
18
19
20
21
22
23
24
25
26
27
28
29
30
31
32
33
34
35
36
37
38
39
40
41
42

Preface

We have used a broad definition of art in these outings. The lines separating art from craft have long ago blurred, and environmental and landscape art have touched the boundaries of architecture. We have similarly tried to include a wide variety of artistic styles, as well as many of the great names of the past and present of our region. In our search for unique sites that have a sense of history or visual appeal or unspoiled charm, we have purposely omitted the more frequented spots. We hope you will not find masses of tour buses or tourist trappings in the places we have selected.

This book is for those of you who have a taste for art and architecture, as well as curiosity for exploring unusual places of artistic interest. You need not be a connoisseur to appreciate the aesthetic pleasures of *Country Artwalks*.

We do not pretend that this is a comprehensive guide to the region's many artistic treats. From the numerous places we visited, we have selected these outings because they captured our imaginations. In your wanderings you might well discover additional places that we would be happy to know about.

In the following pages we will take you on forty-two voyages of exploration into the artists' varied worlds, from the intimate confines of their working studios to the grand sites of their works. These have been outings of discovery for us, as we hope they will be for you.

We call these "country artwalks" because each of our outings has a sense of place, whether as a site for art or for artist. As you walk across a sculpture park, or follow in the footsteps of a landscape painter, or wander through a garden designed after a Chinese painting, we hope you will have a true sense of the artist's space and individual vision.

Our country's artists have historically had a deep and complicated relationship with their land, ranging from romantic views picturing the nation's natural beauty, to abstractions of the landscape, to environmental works in which the landscape itself has become art. These outings will take you, for example, to the panoramic sites of the Hudson River painters, to an environmental artist's quarry sculpture, to two historic cemeteries, or to the homes and studios of some of the nation's most noted artists.

To be an artist in America has rarely been easy. Some have worked together in colonies, like the impressionists of Old Lyme or the abstractionists of East Hampton; others have struggled alone, taking their inspiration from the natural scenery and resources around them. For every illustrious Augustus Saint-Gaudens sculpting at his glorious New Hampshire estate, there have been dozens of artists with creative visions and cold studios tucked away in small towns and rural valleys. We hope art and landscape lovers will enjoy this combination of nature's beauties and artistic creation.

How to Use This Book

Country Artwalks from Maine to Maryland is a special kind of guidebook. It will take you through a large nine-state area, exploring many out-of-the-way places while avoiding well-known urban art centers. It is meant to be a guidebook of artistic discovery rather than a comprehensive listing of every studio and collection throughout the region. With this aim in mind, we invite you to join us in seeking the unusual, inspiring, eccentric, wonderful world of America's artists.

We hope that you will use this book in a variety of ways. Perhaps you will take it along as you travel, choosing a detour or outing not far from your route. Maybe, with the help of our book, you will plan day trips or weekend jaunts to sites of interest to you. Devotees of a particular artist or style of art may choose artwalks relating to their special interest. Even if you live in this region, we doubt you are familiar with all of the fascinating sites in your own state; perhaps our book will guide you to people and places you will want to visit again and again near your own hometown. We have ourselves already used our "finds" to delight foreign guests, to whom vast sculpture parks, for example, are a new and intriguing sight. But perhaps you are simply an armchair reader, content to explore in your mind by reading about distant pleasures. This book is for you, too.

We have divided our collection of artwalks into five sections exploring different aspects of art on site. Our first group of outings follows in the footsteps of American artists, seeking the characteristic—and often magnificent—views they painted. In the second part we visit three sites where you can watch artistic works in progress. Next we take you to a series of wonderful environments: gardens and landscapes both natural and created, places in which nature's beauty has been artistically designed or formalized. The following section includes a series of fascinating visits to the studios and homes of noted artists of the past, locations where some of the best-known American works were made. The fifth and last part introduces outdoor collections in a variety of public settings, ranging from sculpture parks to cemeteries to outdoor museums. You'll find a guide to "choosing an outing" at the end of the book, as well as an index of artists and sites of interest.

We provide you with information about visiting the site and directions at the end of each entry; telephone numbers and Web sites are included when available. It is a good idea to call before you leave home to be certain that the site is open; outdoor art sites may be closed in bad weather. Public places may charge an admission fee, though many are free. We recommend that before setting out you check our occasional "in the vicinity" suggestions at the end of some chapters.

We invite you into the many different worlds of American art and hope our book is easy to use and enjoyable to read. We believe you will savor these artwalks as we have.

In the Artists' Footsteps: Painters' Views of the World around Them

Landscape and History on the Hudson Highlands

West Point, New York

Directions: From New York City, cross the George Washington Bridge and take the Palisades Interstate Parkway north. At exit 15 take U.S. Highway 6 to U.S. Highway 9W north. In the village of Highland Falls you'll see signs for West Point; follow the signs to the visitor center.

The Hudson River painters, the great romantics who glorified America's natural wonders on canvas, were inevitably drawn to the Hudson Valley Highlands. In their quest for what they called the "sublime landscape," they sought vistas that embodied their aesthetic and philosophical ideals. These nineteenth-century artists, who flourished between 1820 and 1880, were dazzled by the scenic grandeur of the West Point region, where dramatic mountain ranges meet the majestic Hudson. Here they captured the spectacular scenery in its many variations.

This is a walk of views and imagination. We will locate some of the sites and vistas the artists immortalized. The actual scenes may not be precisely those depicted in the paintings—artists often use artistic license in their interpretation of nature—but will still be easily identifiable. We will concentrate on four areas, all within walking distance of one another, but you may prefer to drive to and from them and enjoy a walk within each site instead. And if time and energy are no problem, you may also wish to visit additional spots that the artists painted nearby and just across the river.

When you arrive at West Point, you might begin your outing at the visitor center, where you can get a map and other materials. Our first art site is the nearby Regina Hall (once known as the Lady Cliff Building), the single officers' quarters just up the hill from the museum. Though visitors are not encouraged to walk about here (as a sign clearly indicates), a discreet person can take a peek looking south from the river side of the building to the valley below—as we were told to do at the visitor center. The Hudson River master John Frederick Kensett captured this vast panorama in his *View from Cozzens Hotel near West Point* (New-York Historical Society) and no doubt stood on this very spot. Although the Cozzens Hotel is long since gone, the natural landscape remains the same and is as spectacular as ever. Kensett, trained as an engraver, was greatly admired for his muted natural colors and for the atmospheric light and shadows he created in his works. As you can see, this landscape lends itself to his harmonious and almost impressionistic interpretation.

Our next stop is Fort Putnam, high above the West Point campus. To reach Fort Putnam (and you might prefer to drive rather than walk), you must go past the visitor center, continuing straight through Thayer Gate. Proceed left on Mills Road all the way up the hill. Bear left at Michie Stadium and take another left at Delfield Road. You will find a small parking area just below the fort and a little asphalt path leading to it. Fort Putnam can be visited year-round.

It is perhaps most picturesque when the trees are leafy and the river blue, but even if you come during the winter months, you can still walk around it at will and enjoy the spectacular panoramas. There are also walking trails nearby that take you through the woods to the valley below.

Fort Putnam was erected during the Revolutionary War to defend the Highlands at West Point. Called the "Gibraltar of North America," its strategic location made it an important defense site of the region, and its surrender to the enemy the object of Benedict Arnold's treason.

The fort, which could now be described as a "romantic ruin," was a subject that greatly appealed to the Hudson River artists, as can be seen from the number of landscape works it inspired. (In fact, exhibitions of Hudson River paintings frequently include several versions of the same vista.) Its intriguing history, picturesque setting, and extraordinary views made it an ideal setting for artists of the period. Robert Havell Jr. was one of the painters who climbed to Fort Putnam to record its remarkable panoramic view. A native of England who engraved Audubon drawings for a time, Havell turned to painting later on in his career, settling in a home across the Hudson and devoting himself to painting landscapes of the area.

Other views from the same site include Kensett's muted, subtle *View of Storm King from Fort Putnam* (Metropolitan Museum of Art) and John Ferguson Weir's *View of the Highlands from West Point* (New-York Historical Society). Weir—son of Robert Weir, a drawing teacher at West Point, and brother of famed impressionist J. Alden Weir—painted almost precisely the same scene as Havell, but included neither fort nor people. (For more about J. Alden Weir, see chapter 29.)

Storm King Mountain was prominent in many of these landscapes. You should be able to view what those painters saw by scrambling up as high as you can so that the fort is below you, on your right.

From Fort Putnam it's a bit of a drive down to Trophy Point, at water's edge. Find the large parking area nearby and walk east toward the river, to the Kosciuszko Monument off Cullum Road. The well-known monument is easily recognizable, though the top portion was added on after it was painted by the Hudson River artists.

This monument honors engineer Thaddeus Kosciuszko (1746–1817), the Lithuanian-born and Polish-educated who was appointed by George Washington as engineer in the Continental Army to supervise the building of defenses at West Point. In 1828, eleven years after his death, a pedestal and shaft were erected by the academy's cadets on the site of Fort Clinton, the center of the fortifications at West Point. The fort had been strategically located to fire on the enemy during the Revolutionary War and prevent their access to Constitution Island. On this very spot the famous chain was stretched all the way across the Hudson to impede the enemy ships (as is indicated in a commemorative plaque).

You can enjoy a genteel walk by the Hudson shore on a pleasant summer afternoon rather than a bloody event. Look for spectacular vistas from below the monument or from the area around the cannon.

From the monument, continue walking north on the main road to the spectacular overlook for another favorite river scene depicted by Hudson River artists. Looking north, you will see the exact view that Thomas Doughty painted in his *Hudson River near West Point* (Montclair Art Museum). This follower of Thomas Cole was a leading landscape painter in Boston who traveled widely and painted many natural scenes. He has been criticized for not having been a careful enough observer of nature and for having painted from memory all too often. If that is the case, his memory must have been prodigious indeed, for his recording of this view is absolutely accurate.

Though you may be weary from all the walking from one site to the next, we hope you appreciate the inspiration the Hudson River and its surroundings provided for these artists. The river was, in fact, their "muse."

Information: The visitor center at West Point is open daily from 9:00 A.M. to 4:45 P.M. Call (845) 938–2638 or visit the Web site www.usma.edu/visiting.asp.

In the vicinity: There are two additional sites you might want to visit within West Point itself: Flirtation Walk and the Kosciuszko Garden.

While visiting the Kosciuszko Monument, you can take a little detour along the so-called Flirtation Walk (a romantic spot for cadets). A gravel and rock footpath about three-quarters of a mile long, it has the inevitable magnificent views at every turn. From Cullum Road walk down the cliff to the river, past the lighthouse, to the site where the great ship-stopping chain was actually anchored.

Kosciuszko Garden, a pleasant terrace near the south end of Flirtation Walk, was a favorite reading spot of Thaddeus Kosciuszko's. Here he built a little fountain after discovering a living spring. Ornamental shrubs and seats were added later, making this an ideal place for relaxing in pretty surroundings.

Just a few miles away is the incomparable Storm King Art Center sculpture park (see chapter 40).

Of similar interest: Other Hudson River artist sites include Kaaterskill Falls (see chapter 5), Olana (see chapter 27), and Cold Spring, just across the river (see chapter 2). Hudson River painter Jasper Cropsey's house and studio are described in chapter 24.

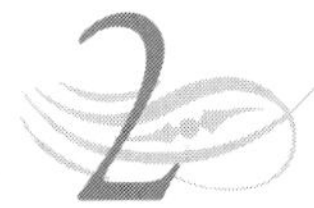

Samuel Colman's Vision of Storm King Mountain

Cold Spring, New York

Directions: From New York City, take the George Washington Bridge to the Palisades Interstate Parkway north to the Bear Mountain Bridge. After crossing the bridge, take Route 9D along the river for 9 miles for a scenic drive to Cold Spring. An alternative route is to take the Henry Hudson Parkway, which becomes the Saw Mill River Parkway, to Route 9D.

One of the most dramatic views of the Hudson Valley is from the village of Cold Spring on the eastern riverbank, looking toward Storm King, the prominent rock-faced mountain on the opposite shore. Storm King's looming presence is always mesmerizing, particularly in stormy weather or at dusk, when light and shadows give it an especially poetic look.

Just as the Hudson River artists chose to paint river vistas from West Point (see chapter 1), they also crossed the river to view the scenery from the opposite side. It was from the small, charming village of Cold Spring that the best views of Storm King could be had. Here, at the foot of the village's main street, was an unobstructed panorama of the river and its mountainous shore.

Among the notable mid-nineteenth-century painters to capture this view was Samuel Colman, a well-known painter of the "second generation" of Hudson River artists. A student of Asher B. Durand, Colman also traveled and studied for many years in Europe, seeking more exotic subject matter. But he is best known for his atmospheric landscapes of Hudson River scenery in both oil and watercolor.

Colman had a successful career, becoming a member of the National Academy of Design and, in 1866, the first president of the American Water Color Society. His luminescent oil painting reflected his skillful enjoyment of watercolor, the medium he preferred during the last twelve years of his life. *Storm King on the Hudson* (National Museum of American Art, Smithsonian Institution) was painted in oil in 1866. Its poetic depiction of the imposing mountain and various boats, dredges, and fishermen on the river is a study in light and atmospheric reflection. (A nineteenth-century critic said that this painting has "some very strong effects of light and shade, and his coloring has a brilliance that is so harmonious as to influence one like a strain of music.") In fact, in works like this one, Colman realized the major objective of so many landscapists of his era: to capture a romantic vision of nature's beauty (with just a touch of industrial progress).

You can see this view across the river to Storm King—and perhaps even a dredge or boat or two—by walking to the end of Cold Spring's Main Street and out to the bandstand at the riverfront at West Street. Choose a day when the sun is breaking through the clouds over the river, and you will not be disappointed by this romantic panorama.

You may also enjoy a brief visit to other sites of interest in this historic village; a small walking-tour flyer is available at many of the little shops. Cold Spring has a long and interesting background as an iron foundry center, and the town is filled with unusually well-preserved old houses dating back to its riverfront prominence as a steamboat port.

Information: The Cold Spring Chamber of Commerce can be reached at (845) 265–3200.

In the vicinity: Just across the river via the Bear Mountain Bridge is West Point, a focal point for Hudson River painters (see chapter 1). Not far from West Point is the Storm King Art Center (see chapter 40).

Of similar interest: Other art sites favored by Hudson River painters are described in a visit to Kaaterskill Falls (see chapter 5).

Modernists in the Adirondacks

Lake George, New York

Directions: To reach Lake George from Albany, take Interstate 87 north (Northway) to the Lake George exit (exit 22) to Route 9N. Continue on Route 9N to Bolton Landing from the town of Lake George.

Lake George, a picturesque spot in New York's Adirondack Mountains, was the inspiration for works by two important modernists: painter Georgia O'Keeffe and sculptor David Smith. On this outing we visit the sites where they worked.

When you think of Georgia O'Keeffe's work, vivid images of nature come to mind—from the sensual flowers and stark animal skulls, for which she is well-known, to her powerful panoramas in which she expresses the physical world in its most elemental form. Though much of her inspiration came from the vast desert landscape of New Mexico, O'Keeffe also lived and painted in New York State.

For years she and her husband, the renowned photographer Alfred Stieglitz, spent each summer and fall on a rustic farm property on Lake George, where her creative output was prodigious. Some of her most abstract works of the 1920s were painted by the lake. She enjoyed the wonderful natural surroundings, turning the landscape around her into abstract shapes and vibrant colors. "Objective painting is not good painting unless it is good in the abstract sense," she wrote. "A hill or tree cannot make a good painting just because it is a hill or a tree. It is lines and colors put together so that they say something . . . the abstraction is often the most definite form for the intangible thing in myself that I can only clarify in painting."

Like many artists before her, O'Keeffe was fascinated by the lake's changing light and movement. The tradition of landscape painting (and beautiful lake views) was well established in the Adirondacks. The unspoiled scenery of upstate New York had long fascinated many painters, ranging from the Hudson River artists to Winslow Homer; it was Georgia O'Keeffe who transformed the prettiness of Lake George into a series of dramatic abstractions.

Drawing on nature as a symbolic representation of inner emotions (she and Stieglitz referred to their nature works as "equivalents"), she turned landscape views into majestic, monumental visions. O'Keeffe spent hours studying the lake under different weather conditions and then painting various abstract versions of the same theme. One of the brilliant studies in this series is *From the Lake No. 1*, painted in 1924 (Des Moines Art Center). Its swirling forms and deep colors create the ominous mood of an impending storm over water. Others in the series are similarly dramatic, with varying colors and symbolic forms.

O'Keeffe's revolutionary contributions to the art of landscape painting are particularly noteworthy if you compare the painting shown here with another view of Lake George by the nineteenth-century artist John W. Casilear, who painted a similar vista in 1857. His canvas, *Lake George* (Brooklyn Museum), views the lake from the southern end; it was a highly regarded painting for its "pure light, neat outline, and distinct grace and grandeur," according to a critic at the time. O'Keeffe's abstract landscapes were seen by many of her contemporaries as equally grand and graceful but by more conservative critics as shocking.

Since the town of Lake George is no longer the quiet little lakeside resort it once was, you may want to travel north and view the lake from a variety of unspoiled locations on both sides. Among them is a particularly pretty spot at Bolton Landing. This small, picturesque village just north of the town of Lake George on the lake's west shore was for many years home to the noted American sculptor David Smith. Smith's whimsical and rhythmic iron works, which he called "drawings-in-space," took American sculpture into new and significant forms. Combining found objects, shapes from the machine age, and free linear patterns, many of Smith's works, such as *Hudson River Landscape* (Whitney Museum of American Art), were loosely tied to the landscape around him. Although the estate with its sculpture-dotted grounds is no longer open to the public, Bolton Landing has for many years been associated with Smith and is well worth a stop. Here you will see a more appealing lakeside village, and perhaps capture something of the aura of the artist's habitat.

If you return several times, you will see the same changing colors and light on the lake and the same unspoiled vistas that inspired these original and independent artists.

Information: The Chamber of Commerce in Lake George can be reached at (518) 668–5755.

In the vicinity: The unusually fine Hyde Collection (161 Warren Street, Glens Falls) is housed in a gracious mansion and includes paintings and sculpture by European and American masters from the Renaissance through the twentieth century. Call (518) 792–1761 or visit www.hydecollection.org.

Of similar interest: You'll find other David Smith sculptures noted in chapters 33, 37, and 40.

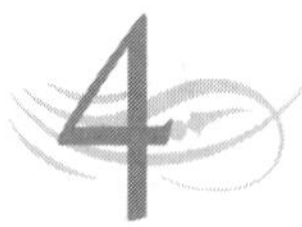

Fitz Hugh Lane, Luminist of the Northeast Seacoast

Gloucester, Massachusetts

Directions: From Boston take Route 128 30 miles north to Cape Ann. Exit 12 will bring you into the town of Gloucester. Pleasant Street intersects Main Street in downtown Gloucester.

Among the prettiest spots on the eastern seaboard is Gloucester on Cape Ann, with its views of the sea, its inlets and bluffs, and its charming houses lining the harbor. Dozens of artists—ranging from the earliest American primitives to John Sloan, Stuart Davis, and Milton Avery—have painted its landscapes and seascapes in their own distinctive styles.

However, no one is more identified with Gloucester than the nineteenth-century seascape artist Fitz Hugh Lane, a native son and perhaps the nation's finest marine painter. It is fortunate for us that Lane's Gloucester paintings are in large part collected in the town itself, and that the sites and vistas that he painted are mostly still there and little changed.

Fitz Hugh Lane was a truly "American" painter of the 1800s,

a luminist to whom the seascape provided an opportunity to convey the beauty of changing light over water. With its emphasis on the atmospheric effects of light in landscapes, luminism was an outgrowth of the Hudson River school of painting and flourished in the mid-nineteenth century. But it was also a different way of seeing not only light but things in nature, a subjective mode of expression that created a mood of tremendous intensity.

Lane's seascapes are startlingly still. Trained as a lithographer, he was a deft and realistic draftsman. He skillfully combined the topographical view—then among the most popular forms of art in America—with a mastery of the nuances of light and sea in different weather and seasons. He combined these carefully observed and recorded panoramas with a delicate stillness, an aura of transcendental peace or arrested time. Lane's paintings show a distinctive and lucid admiration of nature. Some art historians even consider him to have been the visual counterpart of Ralph Waldo Emerson.

Begin your visit in Gloucester at the Cape Ann Historical Association, where you will be able to view some of the forty Lane works it houses and view a half-hour film about the artist. Pick up a map and set out on a walk to find the sites of some of the views he painted. Though Lane was crippled (probably by childhood polio), he worked from a wide variety of locations.

Your first stop is Lane's house, on Harbor Loop atop a hill in the park at Duncan Point. Built of granite blocks in 1849, this house has had a number of lives, including a stint as a jail; it is known as the Old Stone Jug. Lane's studio was on the top floor, from which he could see the harbor. The house is not open to visitors.

Next, make your way to Stage Fort Park, where Gloucester's earliest settlers are supposed to have landed in the 1620s. This site is the subject of several of Lane's paintings. You will see Stage Fort

Park from another vantage point when you visit the former site of Brookbank, the Sawyer homestead (now gone). In Lane's view, which almost seems to be seen by the artist through glass, you can spot Stage Fort Park (left), Gloucester (center), Ten Pound Island and lighthouse (near right), and Dolliver's Neck (far right).

Rocky Neck, the oldest continuous art colony in the country, is another Lane site, as well as a spot frequented by many other artists attracted by its view of the busy harbor. Farther out of town are a series of beaches, including Good Harbor Beach, that Lane used for outdoor sketching and panoramas of the sea.

There are several other Lane sites that the Historical Association can suggest to you, including a place called "Norman's Woe" and a spot along the Annisquam River at the drawbridge. A particularly pleasant way to see his subjects is by harbor boat; Lane was an avid sailor who toured up and down the coastline, sketching. You can arrange such a tour with one of the whale-viewing boats in town.

Also in Gloucester are three other sites of interest that may be visited as you walk through town. The Sargent-Murray-Gilman-Hough House at 49 Middle Street was built by Winthrop Sargent in 1768; it eventually became the home of the daughter of the noted American painter John Singer Sargent. You will find some of his paintings hanging here, along with much to interest historians and architectural buffs as well.

The Hammond Museum at 80 Hesperus Avenue is one of those Renaissance/Gothic-style castles that can frequently be found in unlikely places in the United States. This one contains many fine European design elements, including a fifteenth-century Spanish tile ceiling, a fourteenth-century Italian bed, a Great Hall and a Gothic Room, and a Renaissance-style courtyard and reflecting pool. The museum is also home to one of the greatest Hammond organs in the world; it has 10,000 pipes and 144 stops. Well-known organists occasionally give concerts here.

Beauport, the Sleeper-McCann House, on Eastern Point Boulevard, is another large castle-style mansion that invites visitors to tour its forty rooms. Each of these interiors is a replica of a different era of American design and architectural style, with an emphasis on the eighteenth century.

Information: The Cape Ann Historical Association is located at 27 Pleasant Street, Gloucester. Call (978) 283–0455 or visit www.cape-ann.com.

The Hudson River Painters at Kaaterskill Falls

Kaaterskill, New York

Directions: From New York City take the George Washington Bridge to the Palisades Interstate Parkway to the New York State Thruway north. Exit at Saugerties (exit 20). Take Route 32 to Palenville, then Route 23A toward Haines Falls. After about 3.5 miles you'll see a small sign on the right-hand side of the road indicating the way to Kaaterskill Falls (you will also see a gorge and another waterfall). Go another 0.25 mile until you reach a parking area on the left side of the road. Walk down to the sign indicating the ascent to the falls. All other sites in Catskill State Park are marked.

There is probably no area in the East that has been so immortalized by artists as the Hudson River Valley and the Catskill Mountains area nearby. Fortunately, much of its glorious scenery remains unspoiled and open to the adventurous walker. In fact, a hike to the sites so beloved by Hudson River painters is an experience in both natural and artistic beauty not to be missed. Once you leave your car, you will feel as though you are treading on the same paths and seeing the same views of a century or more ago. And when you come upon these marvelous vistas, you will understand why the

Hudson River artists were so inspired and why American landscape painting caught the attention of the world.

"Nature has spread for us a rich and delightful banquet. Shall we turn from it? We are still in Eden; the wall that shuts us out of the garden is our own ignorance and folly." Thomas Cole, America's first important landscapist, wrote these words in his 1835 "Essay on American Scenery." His colleagues described the natural beauty of the Hudson Valley as evidence of "the hand of God" in the glories of America. This combination of religious exaltation and nationalism characterized their enthusiasm for thc unspoiled wilderness scenery and added immeasurably to the nineteenth-century American perception that this was a golden land with a special destiny.

As artists packed their easels and paint boxes to set out for the countryside, a new appreciation for nature—and for works done at the scene itself—took hold. A loosely knit band of painters became known as the Hudson River school, though there was no actual school involved. While it paralleled the French interest in landscape (exemplified by the Barbizon school) and the romantic realists of England, the Hudson River school was quintessentially American—an attempt to capture the very spirit of the nation. Even the experience of nature became important, as the artists trudged up mountainsides or paddled canoes into the forests to "catch" in sketchbooks or on canvas the wilderness unspoiled. (And soon a typical—and lasting—American debate over progress versus unspoiled scenery ensued. For another view of this issue, see chapter 6.)

Though the Hudson River painters eventually spread their wings and explored New England and other regions, most began their outdoor painting in the Catskill Mountains region and along the great river's banks and bluffs. The area they chose lies along

Kaaterskill Creek, a meandering stream that makes its way between rolling mountains just above the Hudson Valley.

A winding mountain road known as the Rip Van Winkle Trail (you can now drive most of the way) leads to Kaaterskill Clove, the site of many well-known paintings. (*Clove* means "ravine" or "gully," from the Dutch word *cleft*.) Here—at the scenic convergence of narrow gorge, winding river, magnificent trees, and jutting rocks—Asher B. Durand painted his *Kindred Spirits* (National Gallery of Art, Washington, D.C.), probably the most famous Hudson River school painting of all. (Other views of this spot include Thomas Cole's *The Clove, Catskills*, in the collection of the New Britain [Connecticut] Museum of Art, and *Kauterskill Clove* by Sanford Gifford, in the Metropolitan Museum of Art.)

But even more dramatic vistas brought the artists to this region. At the top of the craggy mountains were both a miraculous waterfall and thrilling panoramic views of the Hudson Valley. The area was "discovered" (along with the Hudson River "school") by Thomas Cole in 1825, when he made a rewarding sketching trip to the region. He returned to the city, and his works were shown in a Manhattan shop. Col. John Trumbull, president of the American Academy of Fine Arts; the portraitist and writer William Dunlap; and Asher B. Durand, soon to be a leading landscapist, came upon Cole's paintings.

"This youth," said the illustrious Trumbull, "has done what I have all my life attempted in vain." And the poet and journalist William Cullen Bryant summed up the artistic community's admiration at seeing Cole's Kaaterskill pictures: "Here . . . is a young man who does not paint nature at second hand . . . here is American nature and the feeling it awakens."

Soon other artists were following Cole's lead to the Catskills and to the discovery of nature as a subject. Many of them came to stay at the Mountain House hotel, a legendary inn atop a craggy site near the spectacular Kaaterskill Falls. Taking a train from New York City, the artists could disembark quite near the falls or take a horse and buggy to sketch them up close. (We took a footpath, which is clearly indicated, since conservationists have rightly closed public roads into this wilderness.)

They found Kaaterskill Falls a magical spot, with a two-part cascade over a rosy stone mountainside. Unlike the great falls at Niagara, Kaaterskill seems a private place, hidden deep in the forest, exciting to discover. Its colors, delicate rippling fall, and the spectacular foliage around it have made it one of the most famous American landscape subjects.

On this outing you will also find a spot known as Artist Rock—another grand view that must have enthralled the painters. Here, high above the Hudson Valley (you can see the river below), is a vista that literally takes your breath away. It is, fortunately, easy to reach along a comparatively flat path that winds through exquisite woods and rocky outcroppings. You will easily imagine the artists setting out from the Mountain House, sketchbooks in hand, to record this scenic wonder.

The Mountain House—once an elegant columned inn—is no longer there. Like so many spots made famous by artists, it eventually became too expensive for them, and a few bought homes in the area instead of staying there. It has long since disappeared, and now its dramatic location remains free of buildings. You can walk to the site and look out over the magnificent landscape, with the Hudson a bright ribbon of light in the distance, while massive trees and rocky crags spread out below you—a panorama just as it must have looked to the painters who congregated on the hotel's grand terrace.

In the following paragraphs we will take you on a three-part walk to explore some of the most beloved scenes of the Hudson River painters. This outing can be divided into separate walks, for some of it is rough going, while in other places you can drive to level terrain and walk easily along a flat path. Some of the sites painted by the Hudson River school are now unreachable, including about a quarter mile of the Escarpment Trail that the artists once took from the Mountain House across the mountain to the top of the falls. But many of the locations seen in their paintings are easily accessible to walkers. In each of these sections we will point out the settings for the artists' works; this is one of those rare outings where time and progress seem to have spared the unspoiled beauty of the scenery.

This excursion, being one of our more rugged outings, is recommended for fit walkers in sturdy shoes. Bring along drinking water; you will not find refreshment stands in this wilderness! We recommend the fall foliage season as the best time, when the scenery is unsurpassed. Early summer is also very lovely, but try to go on a weekday if you want total solitude, for hikers and campers know this route. Do not try this outing in winter or early spring because of wet and muddy trails.

Park your car at the public parking area on Route 23A, about 3.5 miles after leaving Palenville and Route 32. Walk downhill about 0.25 mile to a small bridge overlooking Kaaterskill Creek and Bastion Falls, which are quite pretty and worth a second glance. You will see a smallish sign indicating Kaaterskill Falls to be 0.5 mile up from there. (We should add that it's a very long uphill 0.5 mile! Remember, the artists came by buggy above the falls.) Before you set out, cross the road to see a wonderful view of Kaaterskill Clove, perhaps one of the same views admired and painted by the artists.

Start your walk uphill, following the rather sporadic yellow trail markers, which lead you more or less parallel to the creek all the way up to the falls. (If you lose sight of the trail markers, which is likely, just keep walking alongside the creek and you won't get lost.) The going can be quite arduous, as the "path" (which can hardly be called one in some places) has been eroded and footing is uneven. You will be clambering over large rocks, twisted tree roots, and decaying branches and leaves, which may be slippery. The seat of the pants is a good way to negotiate the worse of these hazards. Even though the distance is short, the trek will be difficult for those who are not in fairly good physical condition, who might prefer parts two and three of this walk. (We saw some poor souls trying to negotiate their climb on all fours, and one in high heels!)

But your efforts are well rewarded. The forest is dense with hemlocks and many deciduous trees that are brilliant in fall and romantically green in spring and summer. As you make the rugged but exhilarating climb, you feel somewhat like an explorer in a primeval forest. Finally, you reach a large boulder in the middle of the creek bed from where you get a full front view of the falls in all their splendor. And what majestic falls they are! At 260 feet, they are the highest in New York State (including Niagara Falls, which, of course, are much broader).

The two slender and elegant cascades are divided by a rock basin and surrounded by a landscape that is wild, rugged, and unspoiled. This is a truly romantic scene that any landscapist would adore. If you climb slightly higher, you'll see the spot from which Thomas Cole's well-known *Falls of Kaaterskill* (Westervelt-Warner Museum of American Art, Tuscaloosa) was painted.

After you have stopped long enough to rest and take in this marvelous place, you must retrace your steps. If you have the energy to explore the second section of our artwalk, return to your car to drive up to the North Lake State Campsite, a park from which you can walk to the site of the Mountain House inn. To reach the park from Route 23A, continue in the same direction to Haines Falls and take a right on Route 18, following signs for the North Lake State Campsite. You will arrive at a toll booth where you pay a small fee and are given a map and trail guide that shows you (more or less) how to find the site of the old Mountain House.

Continuing in your car, you now enter Catskill State Park, a woodsy region popular with campers and hikers and filled with clearly marked trails. Park at North Lake, where the road ends. Here you'll see a small sandy beach, picnic and restroom facilities, and signs telling you what is prohibited (nearly everything except hiking). To reach the Mountain House site, follow the signs up a gentle hill until you come to the commemorative marker for the hotel. Continue toward the escarpment for what has been—and you'll find *still* is—one of the most impressive and vast panoramas in the East. The landscape seems to go on forever: Miles of the glistening Hudson are laid out in front of you, surrounded by the lush river valley. On the horizon you can see the Taconic and Berkshire Mountain ranges.

If you walk farther along the escarpment, you'll find a path leading toward Artist Rock (about 0.5 mile away), the third leg of our artwalk. Follow the signs to Artist Rock, Sunset Rock, and Newman's Ledge, trails all quite clearly marked with blue blazes. Once you are past picnic areas and other indications of organized parkland, you find yourself on virgin, somewhat hilly terrain along the cliffs. The views are extraordinary.

It is along this trail that you can look back toward the Mountain House site to see another captivating panorama that inspired so many artists. As you walk, you'll be able to identify the site chosen by Hudson River artist Jasper Cropsey in his painting *Catskill Mountain House* (Minneapolis Institute of Art) in 1855.

Another painting of the same site is Thomas Cole's A *View of the Two Lakes and Mountain House, Catskill Mountains, Morning, 1844* (Brooklyn Museum).

After a short but arduous climb on top of large boulders (fortunately not near the edge of the cliff), you reach a plateau that almost appears to be a man-made terrace, so regular is the rock surface. But this is a natural stone formation; at the top, overlooking the vista beyond, is Artist Rock. The trees around it are overgrown now, but the artists of a century and a half ago could see the Mountain House from here, too. You can continue along this trail to see the wonderful Sunset Rock and Newman's Ledge.

If you are still able and adventuresome, go back to the hotel site and set out on the other section of the Escarpment Trail. It used to be possible to reach the falls from above, along a network of trails that still exist. This extensive trail system includes miles of fabulous views atop tall cliffs overlooking the Hudson Valley and Kaaterskill Clove. The hike from the hotel site to the falls is about 4 miles, but the trail along the ledges is difficult and dangerous. The section of it that actually goes to the falls was recently definitively closed as unsafe, so your walk will not reach the falls from above. Still, you will certainly not be disappointed by the spectacular views.

Of similar interest: Other sites favored by Hudson River painters are described in chapter 1 (West Point) and chapter 2 (Cold Spring). A visit to Thomas Cole's house is included in chapter 27, and a visit to Jasper Cropsey's house and studio is described in chapter 24.

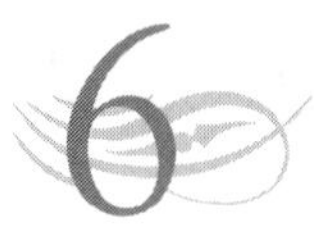

Starrucca Viaduct: Progress amid Natural Beauty

Susquehanna Valley, Pennsylvania

Directions: From New York City take Interstate 80 west to the exit for Route 380 north, which will take you to Interstate 81 north. Exit at Route 171 for the town of Susquehanna.

Hudson River school painters brought the beauty of the American landscape to the attention of a nation that had greatly overlooked it. In their rush to build and develop the country, Americans had paid little attention to their native scenery. The first Hudson River painters spoke in religious terms of "God's hand" in the American landscape and of the duty of all to preserve it. They were, of course, talking about the rivers and hillsides and forests unspoiled by human hands. Their paintings of these glorious views became the first "native" style of painting.

Jasper Cropsey was one of the leading landscapists in this mid-nineteenth-century tradition. A critic at one of his exhibitions remarked: "The axe of civilization is busy with our old forests, and artisan ingenuity is fast sweeping away the relics of our national infancy . . . Yankee enterprise has little sympathy with the picturesque, and it behooves our artists to rescue from its grasp the little that is left, before it is ever too late."

But in a curiously American twist, landscapists soon sought to find a balance between progress and natural beauty. Why not find beauty in man's creations on the landscape as well? In 1865 Cropsey painted *Starrucca Viaduct* (Toledo Museum of Art), a poetic landscape of Pennsylvania's Susquehanna River, including its newly constructed railroad viaduct with a rushing train. To Cropsey, a specialist in fall coloring and naturalistic scenery, the inclusion of a great engineering feat like the Starrucca Viaduct and a steaming train in a landscape was an implicit celebration of American progress.

Cropsey was born in 1823 in New York State and practiced as an architect before leaving for Europe in 1847. Over the next fifteen years, he spent a great deal of time in London, where he was associated with pre-Raphaelite landscapists and the British critic John Ruskin. When he returned home after the Civil War, he continued to paint realistic landscapes, varying his style very little. His specialty was autumn foliage and Eastern scenery. *Starrucca Viaduct*, more than any other of Cropsey's work, captures nineteenth-century America's dual romance with nature and progress.

The Starrucca Viaduct, by the way, was a widely heralded achievement in American engineering. Constructed in 1847–48 by the Erie Railroad, it is the oldest stone railroad bridge still in use in Pennsylvania—and it's a monumental sight to see. At 1,040 feet long, 100 feet high, and 25 feet wide, its massive but artistically arched design is still striking today.

Fortunately for walkers, there is an uncommonly lovely way to see the viaduct and to spot the very site of Cropsey's painting. (Keep in mind that in those days, artists still worked—or at least sketched—out of doors.) We believe that this artwalk will take you to the view that the artist saw along the Susquehanna's charming banks. The walk there, which is less than a mile long, is in itself a delight, and the sighting of the viaduct is both romantic and dramatic.

Begin your walk by leaving your car at the small shopping center behind the First Methodist Church at the intersection of Routes 92 and 171 and Erie Street in the town of Susquehanna. (The painting is subtitled "In the Susquehanna Valley near Lanesboro, Pennsylvania"; you will be walking toward Lanesboro.)

Walk through the parking lot behind the stores. You will see the river and the railroad tracks. Cross the tracks carefully (they are occasionally still in use), and you will find a wonderful riverside path heading to the right (as you face the river). We took this walk in the dead of winter, and it was glorious—both because the view was so clear and because it was deserted, with only a few human and canine footprints in the snow—but you will enjoy the scenic river with its inlets and shoals and leaning trees in any season. You will need to walk less than a mile for your first view of the viaduct towering above the river. At a certain point, which we leave you to discover, you will find yourself in the artist's footsteps.

After your walk, you should drive up the hill (along Route 171) for another view of the viaduct, and if you continue a mile or two farther, for a ride under its massive arches.

Offshore Art Colonies

Appledore, Deer, and Monhegan Islands, Maine

Directions: From Boston take Interstate 95 north, then:

For the Appledore Island ferry take exit 7 (Portsmouth, New Hampshire) to the Shoals Marine Lab dock at 315 Market Street. Call (607) 255–3717. For Deer Isle at Augusta take Route 3 east to U.S. Highway 1 north, then take Route 15 toward Stonington. You can reach the island by car. For Monhegan Island take the exit for Brunswick to US 1 north; at Thomaston take Route 131 south to Port Clyde for the ferry.

Getting away to an island retreat is an enduring popular fantasy. Three enticing islands along Maine's rugged coastline—Appledore, Deer, and Monhegan—have particularly appealed to artists, art lovers, and nature enthusiasts over the years. All provide a pleasurable day's "escape" off the beaten track.

Appledore Island

To visit Appledore is to relive a fascinating period in the American art scene. The ninety-five-acre island, the largest of the barren and somewhat bleak Isles of Shoals, located some 9 miles off the coast of

Portsmouth, New Hampshire, is the site of a beloved Victorian garden that was immortalized in many paintings and writings. One of the first seaside summer resorts on the East Coast during the mid- to late nineteenth century, Appledore has an intriguing history. How this garden was created, how it inspired an entire generation of American artists, and what became of it all add to the lore and appeal of the island.

As early as the sixteenth century, European fishermen found the tiny cluster of islands to be rich fishing grounds, and they colonized them. A thriving fishing industry, unrivaled in New England, brought wealth to the Isles of Shoals for a brief time. After years of neglect, the islands enjoyed a renaissance when summer tourists rediscovered them in the mid-nineteenth century. They liked the romantic, rugged, moorlike beauty of the windswept landscape and ocean views they found there. Thomas Laighton, a businessman from Portsmouth, opened the Appledore House Resort in 1848 to immediate success. With him came his family, including his remarkably creative and charismatic daughter, Celia.

The reputation of Celia Thaxter (her married name) as a poet of distinction grew. She attracted the attention of many of the literary and artistic lions of her time, who became her friends and later visited her at Appledore in the summers. These luminaries—the list reads like a cultural who's who of late nineteenth-century America—included James Russell Lowell, John Greenleaf Whittier, Nathaniel Hawthorne, Harriet Beecher Stowe, Mark Twain, and the painters William Morris Hunt and Childe Hassam, to name a few. They were drawn to the island's stark, wild beauty, true, but especially to the intellectually and culturally stimulating atmosphere Celia provided and to the enchanting flower-filled lifestyle they could enjoy at the hotel. They were also charmed by the fabled garden she cultivated on a terrace that sloped from her cottage toward the sea. This splendid 50-by-15-foot plot of brilliantly colored old-fashioned flowers—poppies, hollyhocks, and larkspur, among many other varieties—contrasted sharply with the harsh, stark surroundings of rocks, brush, and sea, a contrast that greatly struck many of these artists.

One artist who was particularly inspired by Celia's garden was the impressionist Childe Hassam, who painted it over and over in its many configurations. He and Celia became fast friends and collaborators. When Celia wrote an account of the joys and frustrations of creating a garden in a physically difficult environment in *An Island Garden*, Hassam illustrated it. He joyously depicted the vitality and sparkle of her garden and other views of the Isles of Shoals in hundreds of oils, watercolors, and pastels over a period of more than thirty years. Some of his best, most vigorous work—such as his *Poppies on the Isle of Shoals* (Brooklyn Museum) or *Garden in Its Glory* (National Museum of American Art, Smithsonian Institution)—was made during his time at Appledore.

Celia Thaxter died in 1894 and, with her, her offshore cultural salon and lovely garden. The hotel and her cottage burned down in 1914, and Appledore was almost forgotten. During World War II the island housed a submarine observation post (a U.S. Army barracks was placed right on what had been Celia's garden) and, finally, in the 1960s, the Shoals Marine Laboratory, which still exists. In the process of restoring some of the old cottages and building new ones, the laboratory's directors had the imagination to reconstruct Celia's unique garden, using her book as a guide.

The garden has now been restored to include more or less everything Celia grew. It can be enjoyed during the summer months by members of the scientific community as well as by day-trippers.

While on Appledore you should also visit the Laighton family cemetery, a lonely, windswept spot located near the garden; it is here that Celia was buried. Day visitors may ask for permission to tour the classrooms and labs of the Shoals Marine Laboratory, and they can also walk along nature trails to spot gulls, snowy egrets, black-crowned herons, or the other hundred or so species found on the island during migrations.

Getting to Appledore requires some planning and money, but we hope you will feel that being on this special site, with its melancholy beauty and connections with the past, will be inspiring enough to make it worth the effort.

Visitors to Appledore are first taken to nearby Star Island (also a conference center), where there are additional places of interest to see. Don't miss the lovely stone meetinghouse built in 1800, which Nathaniel Hawthorne greatly appreciated, or the Charles F. Vaughn Memorial Cottage with its exhibits of Celia Thaxter memorabilia. Nature lovers can walk along the island's rocky coves and cliffs and hope to spot nesting gulls. Be sure to avoid nesting areas during spring and early summer, however; gulls can be quite ferocious and will dive at those who come too close to their nests!

Deer Isle

In the heady days of early abstractionist painting in America—beginning in the second decade of the twentieth century—such artists as Marsden Hartley, Georgia O'Keeffe, and John Marin all painted in Maine in the summertime. Just as the delicate gardens of Appledore appealed to the impressionists, the more elemental natural scenery of the Maine coast and its islands captured the attention of these painters. The dark pines, jagged rocky coast, and brilliant light inspired such artists to abstract from nature, creating new styles of landscape.

John Marin's paintings of Maine scenery both in oil and watercolor are particularly well known. It is hard to look at Maine's coastline and not see a Marin of the scene in the mind's eye! His summer headquarters were for many years at Deer Isle, about halfway up the Maine coastline. Here he made numerous sketches and paintings of the sea and the land.

Critics have found Marin's work in the twenties and thirties hard to define; they have variously described his style as related to that of Sung Dynasty landscape painting, as an outgrowth of impressionism, and as an attempt to combine both abstractionism and realistic landscape painting. Whatever its antecedents, however, Marin's free use of loose impressionistic images and abstract patterns was very much his own and surely captured the essence of Maine's beauty.

From Deer Isle two other tiny islands off the coast can be seen. *Mark and Andrews from Deer Isle* is a typical Marin watercolor of Maine scenery. You can see this view by crossing the bridge from Sedgewick and proceeding out to Deer Isle by car and then walking to the coast.

Monhegan Island

Monhegan Island has long been known as an art colony. Though its prominence in the world of art is in the past, it is still home to many artists and art lovers. The tiny island—little more than 1 square mile in area—was discovered by seafarers and explorers centuries ago, but it was not until the 1870s that the first artists made the 10-mile crossing from the mainland to paint its wild shores and stormy seas. They were not only drawn to the majestic 160-foot cliffs and dramatic ocean views, but also to the picturesque fishing community, pretty meadows, and virgin forest. (Winslow Homer was a notable exception to the long list of distinguished artists who came and stayed; after experiencing violent seasickness on the ferryboat crossing, he was forced to turn back, never to return!)

Since the late nineteenth century, more than 300 artists, including many notable American painters, have worked on this island. Well-known paintings of Monhegan Island were made by Robert Henri, Edward Hopper, George Bellows, and Rockwell Kent. You may be particularly familiar with Kent's jagged rock forms in his black-and-white woodcuts, or Henri's bold canvases depicting the turbulent and angry sea crashing dramatically against the fish houses on shore. German-born Emil Hozhauer painted the enduring subjects of fishermen with their nets at sea, and, more recently, Jamie Wyeth has depicted the many people and animals that have fascinated him on the island.

A handful of artists still live on Monhegan year-round, although their names may not be as familiar. The majority come to work during the summer months, and, happily for interested art lovers, a few set aside a day here and there for visitors to come to their studios. Inevitably, tourists and day-trippers have discovered the island as well, and they come to enjoy the local art scene—the artists' studios, galleries, and occasional local art exhibits—as well as the little fishing and lobstering village and the many natural wonders. Bird-watchers might spot some of the 250 or so species that stop during spring and fall migrations, and nature enthusiasts can walk the 17 miles of woodsy trails to admire the more than 700 different kinds of wildflowers that bloom in season.

Not surprisingly, the summer months see quite a number of day-trippers, eager to enjoy a few hours on the island before taking the ferryboat back to the mainland. Fortunately, the provident islanders have tried to preserve the natural surroundings as best they can: The atmosphere is noncommercial and tourist facilities are limited, discouraging mass tourism. You must definitely plan to reserve your place on the ferryboat ahead of time, as space is limited.

Before you set off on your day's exploration of art sites on Monhegan, you should get a map at an island shop. Note that the souvenir map showing artists' studios is not necessarily accurate or up to date; to visit the studios open to the public, check the bulletin boards around the village for a flyer indicating visiting times and locations. In some cases you might find signs next to the studios announcing they are open.

On your wanderings don't miss the Monhegan Museum, located in the house formerly occupied by the lighthouse keeper. Here you'll find displays of island flora, birds, geology, and history. There is also an annual art exhibit featuring Monhegan artists.

Information: For Appledore Island the ferry for day-trippers (one hundred visitors maximum per trip) sails out of Portsmouth, New Hampshire, at 11:00 A.M., arriving first at Star Island at about noon; from there you are picked up by the Shoals Marine Laboratory launch for the short trip to Appledore. (You must phone ahead to reserve the launch: 603–862–2994.) The ferry leaves Star Island at 3:00 P.M. for the trip back to the mainland, so those going on to Appledore have less than three hours to visit. The cost of the ferry is moderate, but we thought admission to the garden was expensive. The garden is open on Wednesdays during the summer and can be seen only by guided tour.

For Monhegan Island the ferry leaves from Port Clyde or Boothbay Harbor, Maine, from mid-June to mid-October. Phone (207) 372–8848; write Monhegan Boat Line, P.O. Box 238, Port Clyde, ME 04855; or go to www.monheganboat.com.

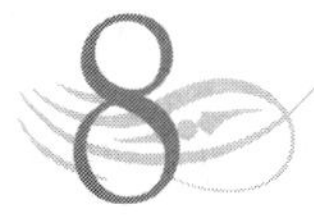

Grandma Moses in Rural New York

Eagle Bridge, New York

Directions: From New York City take the Taconic State Parkway to its end, then the New York State Thruway to Route 22 north, to Route 7 to Bennington, Vermont. From Albany, New York, take exit 23 on the New York State Thruway to Route 787 north to Troy, then take Route 7 east to Vermont, where it becomes Route 9 to Bennington. If you prefer to start your outing at Hoosick Falls, New York, follow the above directions to the intersection of Routes 7 and 22 before reaching the Vermont line.

The pretty rolling landscape of the New York/southern Vermont border will remind you of the picturesque scenes painted by Grandma Moses, the chronicler of a folksy and charming rural America. And no wonder! This area around Eagle Bridge and White Creek, New York (just over the border from Bennington, Vermont), is where she lived and what she painted. She began to paint in 1937, at the age of seventy-seven. Come with us—by bike, on foot, or even by car—on a charming tour of this unchanged and delightful scenery.

This is such picture-book country (and the images of

Grandma Moses are so indelibly engraved on our minds) that we feel nature is once again imitating art. There are bright red barns and stark white houses, black-and-white cows everywhere, old trees and stone walls, astonishingly thick forests outlining the gentle hillsides, and everywhere vistas of Vermont's mountains in a distant lavender haze. In spring and summer the view is startlingly green with spots of yellow and white wildflowers; in fall there are the deeper gold and red tones of the foliage of sugar maple and golden oak; in winter brilliant snowy white fields contrast with black tree trunks and deep green pines.

On this outing you'll see many examples of Grandma Moses's work in a local museum (which also contains the very schoolhouse she attended), the house called Mt. Nebo in which she lived, the nearby hamlet of White Creek Center (the subject of one of her pictures), the studio of a fourth-generation Moses also working in a "primitive" manner, and several specific vistas that Grandma painted.

You can begin your Grandma Moses tour at either end of this picturesque path. If you wish to begin at the Bennington Museum just across the border in Vermont, you'll find a number of her works housed there. This is, in fact, the largest public collection of her paintings anywhere. The museum also contains many of her personal belongings, her worktable, paints and brushes, and family photos. In addition—and perhaps of particular interest to children—is the old schoolhouse she attended, which has been lifted intact from nearby Hoosick Falls and set down adjoining the front entrance to the museum.

In the museum shop be sure to buy two small reproductions of her paintings: a postcard of a painting called *Autumn*, a still-almost-accurate color picture of White Creek hamlet (which you will see on your outing), and, in the form of a note card, a color reproduction of a particularly charming site on Route 68 called *White Creek*.

Once you have steeped yourself in her style, you can set out, guidebook and reproductions in hand. If you go on a weekday, there is the likelihood that you will pass hardly another soul or car or truck, adding to your sense of journeying into an almost forgotten American scene. (By the way, Grandma Moses's autobiography, *Grandma Moses: My Life's History*, describing her childhood in Eagle Bridge, gives a delightful picture that fits right in with the images you will see in her paintings and on this outing.)

You may wish to reverse this tour and begin on Route 22 in New York, ending at the museum.

From Cambridge, New York (an old and rather funky town), head south on Route 22 for about 2.5 miles. You'll see a sign reading WHITE CREEK: 5 MILES; slow down, for you will take an immediate left at a small red barn. Here, right after you turn, is the tiny hamlet of White Creek Center (not the larger town of White Creek). The painting that Grandma Moses made of this little crossroads includes the church and the houses and the chickens, but the old barn with its waterwheel is gone.

After you have wandered around the wonderful rural graveyard, continue on the same road and out into the farm country through which Route 68 meanders so prettily. We highly recommend biking along this route; the hills are not bad and the views sensational. About 0.5 mile past the hamlet is one such view on your left.

Some 2 miles along Route 68 you'll see a green sign with an arrow pointing you toward Eagle Bridge. Turn right here for another lovely tour through farm country to reach Mt. Nebo, Grandma's last home and now the home and gallery of the fourth-generation Moses mentioned above, also a folk painter but working in a more commercial vein.

This road to Eagle Bridge, where the Moses homestead sits, is so inviting that it is a pity to find that Eagle Bridge itself (named for its bridge with a prominent eagle on the top) is a rather rundown town. However, Mt. Nebo is a pristine place, looking as if it had stepped right out of the paintings. To find it, note the large Moses family vegetable stand on your left, just after you recross Route 22 en route to Eagle Bridge. Make a left here, and very soon you'll see a sign directing you to the Moses homestead about 0.25 mile beyond.

You may enjoy a visit to the Moses Gallery, though for us it was less the high point of the tour than a reminder of how hard it is to re-create the innocence of original American folk art in today's sophisticated, commercial climate. But the people who work at the gallery were most helpful in directing us to Grandma's original sites, including the vista we have in hand, White Creek. Retrace your steps across Route 22 and back to Route 68, here also called Cobble Hill Road. This time turn right on Route 68 and continue on toward White Creek. You will pass a picture-book place called September Farm on your left.

Just beyond Rice Lane (on the left), you'll see a white house on a hill also on the left. The charming view painted in *White Creek* was made from this Moses relative's home. Looking out from the front of the house over the valley and hills beyond, you'll spot the two farms in the picture (the Walker Farm, left, and the Perry Farm, right) and White Creek itself, where Grandma's grandchildren went swimming. (The creek is only visible nowadays in winter, since trees have grown up along its banks.)

Continuing on your way, you will next go downhill somewhat to the very old town of White Creek, where several historical markers will date the buildings to pre-Revolutionary times. (Grandma's ancestors were among the first European settlers of White Creek.) From here you can pick up Route 67, which will take you across the state line into North Bennington and eventually back to the museum, on Route 9 on the outskirts of town.

In her autobiography Grandma Moses describes how she went about painting: "Before I start painting, I get a frame, then I saw my masonite board to fit the frame. (I always thought it a good idea to build the sty before getting the pig, likewise with young men, get the home before the wedding.) Then I go over the board with linseed oil, then with three coats of flat white paint to cover up the darkness . . . now the board is ready for the scene, whatever the mind may produce, a landscape, an old bridge, a dream, or a summer or winter scene, childhood memories, but always something pleasing and cheerful, I like bright colors and activity . . ."

Information: You can make this tour any time of the year. The Bennington Museum is open year-round, though only on weekends during the winter months. Call (802) 447–1571 or visit www.benningtonmuseum.com for details.

Cape Cod's Mecca for Artists

Provincetown and Truro, Massachusetts

Directions: From Boston take Interstate 93 south to Route 3 to the Cape Cod Canal; take U.S. Highway 6 to Truro and Provincetown at the tip of the Cape.

The uncommon natural light is the first thing the artist notices about the tip of Cape Cod. Artists first came in the late nineteenth century, when outdoor easel painting was new and was nowhere more inviting. And despite the many, many changes of every sort that have come to this extraordinary place over the last century, along with a drastically changed art world, the artists are still coming.

The wonderful clarity of the light, the brilliant colors, the dramatic scenery, the art "scene"—all of these things continue to bring hundreds of artists to Provincetown and its neighbors, Truro and Wellfleet. The qualities that brought artists and art students in droves still remain, though the Cape end's glory days as an art colony may well have passed. But with its exquisite natural beauty of sand and sea, it remains a vibrant, art-filled place to visit.

You'll still find the picturesque fishing boats moored at Provincetown's wharf, the pristine peach tones of the sand dunes (now the Provincelands of the national seashore), the ever-changing greens and blues of bay and ocean, the New England shingled houses, the startlingly white lighthouses against the deep sky, and the stretches of sand flats with their miragelike spots of color in the distance at low tide.

The visitor who wants to experience the full bloom of the summer art scene should be prepared, however, for a honky-tonk downtown in Provincetown (where art comes in many schlock forms as well as in a serious gallery scene) and a touristy local economy. But the serious art world of the Cape end supports the well-known Provincetown Art Association and some seven or eight galleries, while a half dozen more are thriving in Wellfleet. (All galleries welcome strangers to their openings; just walk in and start up a conversation with the nearest artist, who may well invite you to his or her studio.)

The art you will see ranges widely, from the commercial seascape to constructions dripping red paint (a heartfelt show honoring AIDS victims) to examples of every current style known to the New York art world (from which many of these artists emigrate each summer).

If you prefer a quieter visit, come in the "off-season" after Labor Day. Though your artistic choices will be somewhat narrower (some galleries, but not all, stay open year-round), the towns themselves revert to their better winter natures—cold, windy, and very beautiful.

There are several different ways to capture the ambience of Provincetown's rather odd mixture of the awful and the sublime.

Judging by your own tolerance or enjoyment of the awful part, you can stay in the middle of it, or opt for the lovely, quieter East or West End's rooming houses, or just spend a day or two wandering through its historic streets while living decorously "up-Cape." (The tip of the Cape is known as "down-Cape.")

But try not to miss the wonderful natural and aesthetic beauties that have brought so many artists to this spot since Charles W. Hawthorne first opened his studio a century ago. Provincetown at that time had already had its share of colorful history. (The Pilgrims, in fact, landed there in 1620 before giving up on the sandy spit of land and heading across the bay to Plymouth.) When Hawthorne opened his Cape Cod School of Painting in 1899, Provincetown was merely a collection of fishing shacks, its colorful lifestyle already haven driven Truro to separate itself from its uncouth neighbor.

P-town's fishing industry and picturesque charms were Hawthorne's (and his students') favorite subjects. A generation of young painters followed his lead, sketching out of doors (like their European counterparts) and living cheaply among the hospitable Portuguese fishing community.

Writers, too, including Eugene O'Neill, John Dos Passos, Sinclair Lewis, Susan Glaspell, John Reed, and Mary Heaton Vorse (among other well-known literary names), were living here in the years during and just after World War I. (Norman Mailer, Tennessee Williams, and Stanley Kunitz came later.) The first Provincetown Playhouse opened on an old fishing wharf in the summer of 1915.

But it became very much an artists' town. In 1914 the Provincetown Art Association was formed and is still going strong; its historic roster is a who's who of the American art world of the twentieth century. In the early days, following the groundbreaking

1913 Armory Show and the beginnings of modernism, the Art Association solved the increasing divisiveness of abstraction versus traditional painting by presenting two separate shows each summer. Entries to these exhibitions were judged by a jury of well-known artists of each "school."

Cubist Karl Knaths arrived on the Cape in 1919. Artists like Edwin Dickinson, Edward Hopper, and Max Bohm also came, and Niles Spencer worked in Provincetown in the 1920s. Striking a compromise between realism and abstraction that he called "precisionism," Spencer looked down from the hills behind town at the geometric design of Provincetown's clustered houses and churches. "There is realism in the work of abstract artists," he wrote. "The deeper meanings of nature can only be captured in painting through disciplined form and design."

Since then many artists have chosen to work and show in summertime on the Cape; others have settled in year-round. In the forties and fifties, many of the nation's leading abstractionists opened their own studios and/or schools of painting, among them Adolph Gottlieb, Morris Davidson, Hans Hoffman, Robert Motherwell, Chaim Gross, Franz Kline, Boris Margo, Milton Avery, Victor Kandell, Helen Frankenthaler, Sam Francis, and Mark Rothko—the list is an extraordinary one. Some artists worked from the picturesque sights, abstracting shapes and forms of fishing trawlers at the pier, sand dunes, and ocean waves; others enjoyed the art colony's atmosphere while creating purely abstract works.

Your peregrinations in Provincetown should include the Art Association, which still has juried shows as well as a magnificent permanent collection of about 500 priceless works. Here you will get a taste of the great variety and diverse styles the town's artists have produced over the years. While there, pick up painter Ross Moffett's history of the Provincetown Art Association for the complete story of this amazing mix (and nonmix) of creative people within a tiny town on the sea.

As you explore Provincetown you'll also sense the inspiration for many a painting in the sights around you, beginning with the sailboats in the harbor (a beloved subject of semiabstract and cubist painters, with their stark white triangles of sail) and the fascinating complexity of the fishing trawlers, with their orange masts, deep-colored hulls, and nets and ropes and flags. Walk out to the end of the main pier where they are moored to see the inspiration for many paintings.

In addition to the two piers with their fascinating scenes, visit the Town Hall to see Charles Hawthorne's murals of fishermen at work. Climb up Monument Hill for overviews of the town (like the Niles Spencer mentioned above), and wander the narrow streets in both the East and West Ends. Walk across the breakwater and hike across the dunes to the ocean (by beginning just outside of town at the Head of the Meadows) for panoramic views.

Stroll out on the sand flats at low tide or visit the "back beach" (the ocean side), where you'll catch the aura of Milton Avery's beach scenes. The jumble of signs and buildings on downtown's Commercial Street, the strange formations of seaweed at high tide, the curious vegetation in the sand out by the beaches of Race Point or High Head—these are all images that have fascinated artists of many generations working in a wide variety of styles.

Some artists have always preferred the peaceful landscape of Truro to the bustle of Provincetown. Among them was Edward Hopper, who painted many scenes of the oceanfront, including Highland Light (North Truro) and views of the gentler Pamet River area of Truro on the bay side.

And, of course, visit the galleries. Despite the passing of Provincetown's glory days as the center of the nation's new art, there is still lots to see, and you may well discover a painter or sculptor whose work captures for you the very ambience of the Cape and its long artistic history. Only a few major galleries remain in Provincetown; three are in the East End (as is the Art Association). Wellfleet now has a number of top-notch galleries, most within a block or two of one another. Don't miss the distinctive new art being shown there during the summer.

Information: The Provincetown Art Association is at 400 Commercial Street; call (978) 487–1750 or visit www.paam.org. While the height of the summer season is when most galleries are open, many people prefer the off-season for visiting the Cape.

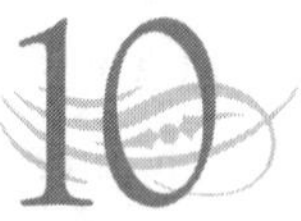

William Sidney Mount, Long Island's Genre Painter

Setauket, New York

Directions: From New York City take the Midtown Tunnel to the Long Island Expressway (Interstate 495) to exit 62. Proceed north on County Road 97 (Nicolls Road) to its end, then turn left onto Route 25A for 1.5 miles to the intersection of Route 25A and Main Street in Stony Brook. Stony Brook is also on the Long Island Railroad. To reach the Hawkins-Mount Homestead: After leaving the art museum, turn left at the bottom of the driveway and go about 0.5 mile to a fork. At the intersection of the fork, you'll see Mount's house and barns immediately on your left. For West Meadow Beach: Continue on Route 25A into the village of Setauket. Take Old Field Road (left) to West Meadow Road, and continue to the beach, from which you can view Crane's Neck as Mount did. To the Mill Dam: Continue on Stony Brook's Main Street from the museums; you will see the mill on your left.

William Sidney Mount was a genre painter and portraitist who cheerfully chronicled rural life in the far reaches of Long Island. A true nineteenth-century American jack-of-all-trades, Mount made paintings, wrote music and played the violin, thought up inventions (including a new kind of fiddle), and left numerous diaries and letters, musical compositions, designs, and—of major interest nowadays—paintings. A visit to his homestead and the surroundings that he painted might give you a taste of a simpler, more contented time, as seen by a talented and pleasing artist.

By the mid-nineteenth century, genre painting—the first truly popular style of art in the United States—had replaced the heroic historical panoramas of earlier Americana. Appealing storytelling scenes of farm life and domestic events, along with character studies, captured the tenor of American life, and beginning in the 1830s were popular with all kinds of just plain folks. Genre artists painted what they knew and saw around them, sometimes adding a touch of whimsy or morality to appeal to the current taste.

But a few of them, like Mount, brought to their work more than sentimental anecdote or sappy romance; in Mount's paintings there is both joy and artistic sophistication. Seeing a collection of his canvases all together (which you will be able to do on this outing) is to experience a full and charming picture of a particular time and way of life.

To Mount, Stony Brook and Setauket, where he lived—and from which he rarely ventured—were not just pretty landscapes. They were places in which real people lived, fished, hunted, danced, and fiddled. Ordinary people were Mount's subjects. "I must paint pictures as speak at once to the spectator, scenes that are most popular, that will be understood on the instant," he wrote. On the other hand, he rejected popularity for its own sake. "I must endeavor to follow the bent of my inclinations. To paint portraits or pictures, large or small, grave or gay, as I please, and not be dictated by others. Every artist should know his own powers best and act accordingly." From these thoughts, we must conclude that he painted what he most enjoyed, and that good humor is evident in his work.

No grand ladies in gilded drawing rooms attracted Mount's brush. Instead, farmers "nooning" or checking the growing corn or making cider, young folks dancing to a jolly fiddler's tunes, neighbors reading the morning paper or holding up a newly trapped rabbit—these were the small daily parts of Mount's warm and wholesome experience. Many of his paintings gracefully include African Americans farming and fiddling and, in one of his best-known portraits, playing the banjo; Mount's were among the first American paintings to do so.

Just as Mount lived his entire life in the same region, in the midst of his apparently jovial family, the greater part of his paintings, journals, inventions, and letters are also still together in one place. In fact, a visit to the museums at Stony Brook will afford a fine sampling of his oils; here you can also see more of the memorabilia relating to his family, who were quite an extraordinary group. If you find yourself thoroughly intrigued by the subject, speak to the curator, who is both available and enthusiastic; a great deal of research has been done on the Mount family, and much of it is published. To some historians the artist and his well-documented life seem to be a shining example of Yankee charm and ingenuity, combined with a successful career as an artist.

The son of an innkeeper, William Sidney Mount was part of a large and cohesive family, many of whom were artists of some sort. One brother was a sign painter who discovered William's talent and sent him for his only formal training—two years at the National Academy of Design. Another brother, Shepard Alonzo Mount, was also a well-regarded portraitist; his sister painted flower pieces. Yet another brother was an itinerant dancing master, to whom William sent tunes and advice, and there were various in-laws and nephews and nieces.

Correspondence with all of these people has been published

in a large book on Mount and, like his painting, shows his warmth and modest disposition. "I yearned to be a painter," he wrote. "I asked God in my humble way to strengthen my love for art; and in His goodness He directed me to a closer observation of nature and I gained strength in art."

Still standing and newly renovated by preservationists is the Hawkins-Mount Homestead, the house in which Mount lived a great part of his life. You can visit the homestead (be sure to see the painting Mount did of it first) and the barns immortalized in so many of his paintings, including *Dance of the Haymakers* and *Dancing on the Barn Floor* (both, The Long Island Museum of American Art, History & Carriages) and *The Power of Music* (Cleveland Museum of Art).

You may also want to drive out to West Meadow Beach to see the view of Crane's Neck, another subject of a Mount painting on view at the museum. The picturesque Mill Dam in Stony Brook was also a favorite Mount site. The mill and large waterwheel at the dam can still be viewed on a nice walk, though the mill itself has been enlarged considerably since Mount painted it.

Information: The Long Island Museum of American Art, History & Carriages (formerly the Museums at Stony Brook) is located at 1200 Route 25A, Stony Brook, Long Island. Open Wednesday through Saturday from 10:00 A.M. to 5:00 P.M. and Sunday, noon to 5:00 P.M. Call (631) 751–0066.

Works in Process: Studios, Workshops, and a Glass Factory

11

Wheaton Village: Historic Glassworks

Millville, New Jersey

Directions: Wheaton Village is in Millville in Cumberland County, halfway between Philadelphia and Atlantic City. From the New Jersey Turnpike, take exit 4 to Route 73 north to Interstate 295 south. Go to exit 27 (Route 42 south), then take Route 55 south to exit 26. Follow the brown signs to Wheaton Village.

Wheaton Village is a celebration and historical evocation of one of New Jersey's most important industries of the past—glassmaking. The first successful glass factory in America was opened in this area by Caspar Wistar in 1739. This industry, which produced bottles and windowpanes for the growing population of colonists, was ideal for the area: Southern New Jersey had abundant fine-grained silica sand and a vast supply of pine wood for the glassmaking furnaces.

Wistar, a native of Germany, arranged with a sea captain to bring trained glassmakers to America from Germany to teach him the secrets of the craft. In exchange Wistar provided the craftsmen with homes, food, servants, and a share of the profits. The factory soon began producing everything from windowpanes and utilitarian bottles to elegant glass ornaments. What became known as "Wistarburg glass" had fine, decorated surfaces with whorls of color or white ornamenting the glass. (In fact, some of the techniques for delicate tinting have never been reproduced.) Wistar's success was so widely known that a highway was built to Millville from Philadelphia to bring visitors to watch the process of glassmaking (much as we can do today at Wheaton Village). Today Wistarburg glass is a collector's item.

Before long, Wistar was joined by numerous other glassmakers who opened their own factories. Although Wistar's factory closed under the watch of his son in 1781, by the late 1800s some seventy other glassworks were functioning in Millville, Bridgeton, and the surrounding area. Numerous waterways allowed for easy transportation of their wares. And by 1854 a railroad was running from the coast to Camden. Not all the glassworks were successful, however. After the Civil War a number of them failed—you can still see the remains of one such enterprise in two ghost towns called Hermann City and Bulltown on the Mullica River. We are fortunate that Wheaton Village has been preserved so that we can get a good idea of what life was like in the many small glassmaking villages of the region.

In 1888 Theodore C. Wheaton, a physician and pharmacist, bought a glassworks in Millville. As a pharmacist he realized the growing need for glass containers, and today Wheaton Village gives us an idea of what the T. C. Wheaton Company and its accompanying village were like a century and more ago. In addition to the factory, there was a full village, with shops, a schoolhouse, homes, and a general store.

Today you can visit the working replica of the factory, where you can watch hot molten glass become a delicate object. In addition you can enjoy a variety of craft shops, ride in a half-scale railroad, and even watch a medicine show. Of major interest is the Museum of American Glass, containing some seven thousand glass items. Wheaton's bustling craft center now includes a variety of shops and demonstrations. The most interesting, of course, is watching glass artisans at work, shaping, blowing, and molding the hot glass with nineteenth-century techniques.

You can stay as long as you like watching the fascination process of glass creation, and you can even chat with the "gaffers" (glass-blowers). You can learn how molding, blowing, and shaping are done, and how colors and bubbles are added. But you need not only be an observer; some of the many craftspersons allow you to participate. The most popular activity among visitors is making paperweights.

Wheaton Village is not only interesting as a craft center and re-creation of a major New Jersey industry of a century ago, but it also reminds us of the way of life in a mid-nineteenth-century rural village, with its one industry, its self-sufficient main street amid surrounding natural beauty. It is the layout of the village, with its long central roadway bordered by great trees, a lake, a traditional village green, and charming small buildings that truly evokes a bygone era.

Carl Sandburg celebrated Millville's glass furnaces in his work "Millville," in which he wrote: "Down in Southern New Jersey, they make glass. By day and by night, the fires burn on in Millville and bid the sand let in the light." Today Wheaton Industries, still a family-owned company, is one of the top glass manufacturers in the world. But their factories have moved into Millville itself, and this romantic small town is a reminder of the growth of American industry from its rustic beginnings to international prominence.

Information: Open seven days a week, April through December, from 10:00 A.M. to 5:00 P.M. Open Wednesday through Sunday during January, February, and March. Closed on major holidays. Many events are scheduled here; call for information. Group or individual tours are welcome. Telephone: 800–998–4552 or 856–825–6800; Web site: www.wheatonvillage.org.

12

Folk Art and Modern Craft Workshops at Peters Valley

Layton, New Jersey

Directions: From New York City cross the George Washington Bridge and take Interstate 80 west to exit 34B. Take Route 15 north to U.S. Highway 206 north, then turn left onto Route 560 west and continue through the blinking light in the center of Layton. Take Route 640 for about 1 mile, and turn right onto Route 615. Go approximately 1 mile and follow the signs to Peters Valley.

To witness the making of an art or craft object is a compelling experience for anyone interested in the creative process. At the Peters Valley Craft Center in rural New Jersey, you can watch a piece of metal, wood, or fabric take on a new identity such as a one-of-a-kind weather vane, a musical instrument, or a wall hanging.

Situated in a remote wooded site within the Delaware Water Gap National Recreation Area, Peters Valley is obviously far removed from the bustling urban scene. Still, this tiny community bursts with the creative energy of the artists and artisans who live and work here. Fortunately, they are willing to share their world not only with the students who come to learn about their art, but also with the more casual visitor who is interested in observing these works in progress.

Peters Valley is a genuine crafts community and not a contrived setup for tourists. Established in 1970 as a nonprofit education center, its role has been to promote traditional and contemporary crafts through a wide variety of programs. Professional artisans (one for each discipline) in blacksmithing, ceramics, fine metals, photography, textiles, and woodworking are selected to live here for one year and manage their own studio with the help of an assistant. In the summer a large and diverse number of artisans come from all over the country to teach inexperienced as well as advanced students. A crafts store displays the work produced on the premises, and an art gallery hosts annual shows. And, of special interest to us, there is the so-called studio interpretive program, which enables the visitor (during the summer months) to see artisans at work in their studios.

A walk through Peters Valley will be a treat not only for those who like crafts, but also for nature lovers, for this is a spot of great beauty. As you wend your way from one studio to the next, you will discover many an inviting path through the woods and might be tempted to wander farther afield into the vast surrounding national recreation area after your visit.

Although Peters Valley is by no means an extensive community, it does include a good number of small buildings scattered about and tastefully integrated into the woods, some almost hidden from view. Not only are there the six main working studios (one dedicated to each craft), but also the Doremus Art Gallery, the Peters Valley Contemporary Craft Store, the Bevans Church (an old frame building sitting prettily behind a quaint graveyard and used for social gatherings), and several dormitory and other service facilities.

To get your bearings, pick up a self-guided walking-tour map at the Peters Valley Craft Store. This is the first building you see when you reach this tiny community after your fairly circuitous route over winding roads—a charming frame house with an old-fashioned porch, directly in front of a most unusual tall house in the Greek Revival style (which turns out to be the photography studio). The store is filled with the works of the on-site craftspersons and is a great place to browse.

Across the street you'll find the Peters Valley office, from which you can get all the information you'll need. You can either walk from one studio to the next on your own or take a guided tour. In the same building as the office, on the second floor, is the Doremus Gallery, which features three annual shows: the Summer Faculty Show, the Studio Assistants' Show, and a show dedicated to works from the anagama kiln behind the ceramics studio.

Before you start out on your studio tour, remember that what you will see at each studio will depend, of course, on the workshops in progress and on the particular area of expertise of the artist on the premises at the time. But we can assure you that you will be treated to a wide variety of techniques and materials of interest to any crafts buff.

Begin your walk at the store, where a small path will lead you to the photography studio, unmistakable with its Greek-columned facade. Here, in addition to the basic developing and printing of black-and-white and color prints, you might chance upon workshops dealing with nineteenth-century platinum/palladium printing techniques or alternative photographic techniques such as infrared film, toning, or hand-applied colors, or you might find discussions on photographic thought and vision.

At the nearby fine metals studio, next on your self-guided walk, you might see anything from silversmithing and metal casting to forging and soldering to jewelry making or designing of metal furniture. At your next stop, the wood studio, you might find an artist at work in the fascinating process of traditional gilding—from the preparation of gesso to the laying and burnishing of gold—or you might see the making of a shoji screen, an acoustic guitar, or even a wooden canoe. Here, the unusual seems usual!

At the textile studio, objects are made from a wide variety of materials using different techniques. You might see individuals at work on vine basketry, tapestry making, paper marbleizing, or silk screening, to name only a few of the possibilities. The ceramics studio is fun to visit, especially if the 50-foot-long anagama kiln is being fired. The six-day firing of it starts with a slow but constant fire and builds up to one in which the temperature reaches an amazing 2,400 degrees Fahrenheit, with smoke and flames surging on all sides. Clay tiles, pottery, ceramic jewelry, and functional pots are among the items made here. At the blacksmith studio you might see the making of a weather vane, forged furniture, or decorative metal objects.

The best time to visit Peters Valley is from June 1 to August 31, when everything is open. You might especially enjoy the annual crafts fair, which takes place during the last weekend of July. Here, again, you can watch a variety of craft demonstrations and browse through the many works on display by some hundred or more artisans. Nature lovers might prefer to come to Peters Valley during the off-season. True, some of the studios and other facilities may be closed to the public, but the woods are quiet and you will have the place almost all to yourself.

Information: Peters Valley Craft Center is located on Route 615 in Layton, New Jersey. It is open seven days a week year-round from 10:00 A.M. to 5:00 P.M., though the studios are only open to the public from June 1 through August 31 on Saturday and Sunday from 2:00 to 5:00 P.M. Guided tours are offered Saturday and Sunday at 2:00 P.M. and leave from the crafts store. The Doremus Gallery is open seven days a week during the summer from 9:00 A.M. to 5:00 P.M., but only on weekdays during the rest of the year. For more information call (973) 948–5200 or visit www.pvcrafts.org.

In the vicinity: The Delaware Water Gap is one of the East's most picturesque spots. Now a national recreational area, it is accessible at many different points for walking and viewing the spectacular vistas. A number of nineteenth-century landscape artists chose this site for painting; among them was George Inness, whose panoramic painting of it can be seen at the Montclair (New Jersey) Art Museum.

Of similar interest: Two other sites devoted to artisans at work are in the region. Historic Sugar Loaf, an "art and crafts village," is a tiny but vibrant community of artisans at work in Orange County, New York (see chapter 13). The Museum Village of Orange County (845–762–8247; www.museumvillage.org) is a large outdoor museum not far from Sugar Loaf (off Route 17 at exit 129) that includes more than thirty buildings housing demonstrations of crafts and early American life.

13

A Crafts Village in the Catskills

Sugar Loaf, New York

Directions: From New York City take the New York State Thruway to exit 16, Route 17 west. Go 8 miles to exit 127, then turn left and follow the signs.

Once a sacred burial ground for the Minisink Indians and then a colonial settlement, Sugar Loaf became known early on as a center for crafts and provisions. By 1830 artisans included a blacksmiths, two cooperages, a cabinet maker, a carpet maker, a tannery, a cheese factory, a wagon maker, and a sawmill owner, among numerous others. Craftspeople continued to work in this small mountain community (named perhaps for its curious bald mountain that reminded colonial settlers of a sugar loaf), but it was only in the 1960s, as the nation experienced a revival of interest in handmade goods, that Sugar Loaf began to draw artisans from around the country.

Today this tiny, vibrant village has become a haven for crafters and the visitors who enjoy seeing them at work and purchasing their wares. Most of the working studios are open to the public. You can visit studios and shops that create everything from leather goods to stained glass, wood designs to handmade candles, pottery to hats and jewelry, musical instruments to rag dolls, and quilts to handmade furniture. More than fifty shops and galleries are presently open.

Known as the "village of craftsmen," Sugar Loaf is an inspiring—and amusing—way to spend a day away. Bring the children! They will love seeing how the many things used daily are made by hand. After your visit to this picturesque Warwick Valley site, you can take the family apple picking at several nearby orchards.

Information: Sugar Loaf is open year-round. Most businesses are open Wednesday through Sunday from 11:00 A.M. to 6:00 P.M. There is a free visitors' guide available at the chamber of commerce. For more information call (845) 469–9181 or go to www.sugarloafnychamber.com.

Of similar interest: Off Route 17 (at exit 129) is the Museum Village of Orange County (845–762–8247; www.museumvillage.org), a large outdoor museum with more than thirty buildings housing demonstrations of crafts and early American life.

Artistic Landscapes: Formalizing Nature

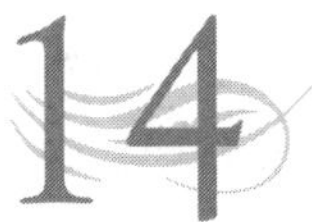

Old Westbury Gardens: Elegance on Long Island

Old Westbury, New York

Directions: From New York City take the Midtown Tunnel to the Long Island Expressway to exit 39S (Glen Cove Road). Continue east on the service road of the expressway 1.2 miles to Old Westbury Road, the first road on the right. Continue 0.25 mile to the garden entrance on your left. The gardens are also reachable via the Long Island Railroad to Westbury from Pennsylvania Station in New York, then by taxi from the Westbury station.

The magnificent black iron gates and the grand allée beyond introduce you immediately to the glamorous ambience of Old Westbury Gardens. Here is the splendor of the magnificent European-style formal gardens of the past, their harmonious elegance graced with outdoor sculpture. This is a great estate on the grand scale, bringing to mind hazy romantic scenes involving Edwardian images and moonlit nights. In fact, the gardens are used frequently for movie sets and picture-book weddings, as well as by historians of landscape architecture of the past.

Just a stone's throw from the ultimate contemporary highway

landscape, this site is all the more intriguing in its contrast with Long Island sprawl. The estate, built in 1906 by John S. Phipps, a financier and sportsman, is not the only grand house in Old Westbury, where many of the rich and fashionable built their homes at the turn of the twentieth century. (Nearby are the William C. Whitney Racing Stables, for example.)

Mr. Phipps hired the London architect George Crawley to construct a Stuart-style "country" mansion, to please his English wife. Westbury House was built atop a hill; its symmetrical elegance is set off by a master plan of landscape design. In fact, the estate is a rare example of landscape and architectural planning that went hand in hand; the complementary designs of the house and its surroundings are worth noting and are of great interest to modern design.

The interior of the house is elegant and formal. It is open to the public and will appeal to those who enjoy seeing how such country retreats were designed and furnished—from fluted Corinthian columns and French windows to polished antique tables and ormolu clocks. You will also find paintings by John Singer Sargent, George Morland, Joshua Reynolds, and Sir Henry Raeburn.

But of particular interest and delight to us were the gardens, which—even without the many sculptures—are a work of art in themselves. Designed by both Crawley and a French landscape architect named Jacques Greber, the master plan called for a formal geometric arrangement of grand allées, softened by English "romantic," or picturesque, gardens. The combination, clearly based on the layouts of the grounds of stately English homes, is an unqualified success.

Among its charms are a lake walk (yes, of course, there is a lake) leading to a "Temple of Love," a boxwood garden, a garden with flowers of all the colors of the rainbow, a "ghost walk" of dark hemlock trees, and a walled garden where you can easily imagine—

or enjoy—the most romantic of trysts. There are numerous rare and magnificent trees and plantings, including many from Asia. Almost 300 species of trees are flourishing at Old Westbury Gardens. Depending on the timing of your visit, you may see profusions of rhododendrons, lilacs, roses, and too many more of nature's most beautiful flowers to list here.

Sprinkled liberally throughout these enchanting areas are neoclassical sculptures and columns and various other artworks that add to the ambience of European elegance. Ceres is sheltered in a pergola of wisteria, while a terra-cotta Diana the huntress graces a curving colonnade within the boxwood garden. There are ornamental cherub fountains in pools of lotuses and lilies; a pair of bronze peacock statues with topiary tails; a shell mosaic in the style of seventeenth-century Italian grotto decoration; a sundial topped with rampant lions; groups of nymphs and satyrs on the roofline of the house; a pair of lead eagles and stone vases on pediments, surrounded by lilacs; and a sculpture of the quasi-mythical athlete Milo of Cortona wresting a tree stump from the earth. You will surely discover additional sculptures tucked away in niches and along walkways.

Old Westbury Gardens are not unknown in the New York area, so we suggest visiting on a weekday if you can. There is a moderate admission charge, and holiday festivities are occasionally held at the estate. You can pick up pamphlets and guides to the garden at the mansion.

Information: Old Westbury Gardens are located at 710 Old Westbury Road on Long Island. They are open May through December from 10:00 A.M. to 5:00 P.M. every day except Tuesday. Call (516) 333–0048 or visit www.oldwestburygardens.org.

15

Monument to the Coal Miners

Frostburg, Maryland

Directions: From Baltimore take Interstate 70 west to Hancock, then take Interstate 68 west to the Frostburg exit (exit 33) and follow the signs to Frostburg State University.

Here in western Maryland's mountainous Allegheny County, the term "environmental art" takes on a new meaning. Deep in the heart of coal-mining country, the artist Andrew Leicester has created a memorial to miners that is truly "environmental."

Western Maryland was the site of the first bituminous coal mines in the country, and the state's arts council decided to commemorate this part of its history with a sculpture on the Frostburg State University campus. Leicester had grander ideas; his work combines sculpture, architecture, painting, and, of course, the environment. It celebrates the uses of the earth, the glories of the natural setting, and the hard life of the miners who worked there. But this is not merely a reconstructed piece of the past; made in 1982, *Prospect V-III* is a contemporary work of art in every sense.

The choice of Frostburg's campus was not an accident. Here,

where miners actually worked, land was purchased in the late nineteenth century for a normal school, with the help of the miners' donations as they left the pits each day. Near the campus is a modern mechanized strip mine, which replaced the shafts and pits used in the past. The contributions and assistance of retired miners in the area are evident throughout Leicester's work; the memorial is a deeply felt tribute to the community, which has responded with enthusiasm.

Prospect V-III is primarily a wooden structure that is 27 feet high and more than 120 feet long. Descending into a shaft deep in the ground, it is designed to bring to mind the architecture of mining shafts and company towns. Its spectacular setting on a steep hillside overlooking picturesque George's Creek is emphasized by a viewing platform at the edge of the construction. (The George's Creek basin was the historical center of early coal-mining operations.)

There are three individual chambers, a hexagonal rotunda, and, at the center of the construction, a realistic, narrow mine shaft that plunges into the earth to an actual coal seam. Each section of this work has its own significance; by utilizing both realistic trappings and conceptual forms, the artist has made an extraordinary monument to an entire industry and its workers.

In the first chamber there are railroad tracks leading to the shaft; on them sits a coal cart that doubles as a cradle. The symbolic butterflies painted on the walls ironically turn into black lungs, in reference to the scourge of "miner's disease." The second chamber is tomblike, representing the miners' deathlike surroundings while they work. A fascinating collection of memorabilia donated by local miners and their families, from lunch pails to picks and shovels to old photographs and documents, adorns the third chamber. This is a most evocative part of the memorial.

The domed rotunda separates the mine shaft from these three chambers. Its skylit ceiling—a surprise after the dark rooms—contains suspended miners' clothing. This display represents the changing rooms, where the workers put on their black overalls to begin their descent into the earth. The walls of the rotunda bear words and symbols ranging from hieroglyphs from the Egyptian Book of the Dead to English mining terms. Half buried in the hillside, the rotunda—with its light ceiling but dark opening toward the shaft itself—accentuates the miner's tomblike experience. Finally, there is the entrance to the shaft, where the tracks vanish into the dark.

Leicester's memorial brings ideas of contemporary art to the public in a strikingly understandable and purposeful way. Its subject was dear to the community, and the work obviously was designed to communicate on many different levels. In the case of this environmental art, there is little question of relevance.

Information: This site may be visited in the spring and fall by appointment only. Call Frostburg State University's (www.frostburg.edu) Visual Arts Department at (301) 687–4797 to arrange your visit.

16

Ladew Topiary Gardens: Plant Sculpture in Eccentric Forms

Monkton, Maryland

Directions: From Baltimore take Interstate 83 north to Interstate 695 west. Take exit 27B (Route 146), cross the bridge, bear left onto Route 146 (Jarrettsville Pike), and travel 14 miles to the gardens.

A fox hunt within the grounds of a formal garden? As unlikely as it may sound, you will indeed find one at Ladew Topiary Gardens in Monkton, Maryland. But instead of a lively scene of red-coated riders and yelping hounds, you'll find a quiet green sanctuary. Fortunately for the potential victim, no real fox hunt takes place here—only a giant topiary version of one.

Topiary art, in which yew and other growing plants are trimmed into artistic shapes and forms, is rare in this country. Though many public gardens clip hedges into pyramids or other geometric forms, a garden of representational topiary shapes is unusual and certainly great fun, particularly for children.

Ladew Gardens were the creation of Harvey Smith Ladew, a prominent and somewhat eccentric New York socialite; he moved to the Maryland countryside to pursue his equally great passions for fox hunting and building gardens. The fifteen gardens that comprise this twenty-two-acre site were recently restored to their former splendor, some years after his death. Filled with surprises at every turn, they reflect Ladew's wit, whimsy, and peculiar interests.

One of the most delightful spots is, unquestionably, the plant sculpture fox hunt tableau, which includes two horses and riders jumping over a fence, following six yew-covered hounds in hot pursuit of a fox. Grassy walks throughout these green acres take you to other topiary delights interspersed among hedges, behind fountains, and around walkways, including a flock of twelve graceful swans "floating" atop a hedge, seahorses, a lyrebird, a Scottie running toward his bowl and ball, and the somewhat incongruous forms of Winston Churchill's victory sign, a Chinese junk, and a large Buddha.

More conventional gardens representing a variety of styles also grace the elegant premises: a carefully tended wild garden (not such a contradiction of terms within this context), an old-fashioned Victorian rose garden enclosed in a circular brick wall, a yellow garden, white garden, water lily garden, iris garden, and even a Garden of Eden, with a statue of Adam and Eve surrounded by azaleas and apple trees. A terrace garden features steps flanked by topiary obelisks in formal rows. A Temple of Venus (Ladew's "folly" perhaps) overlooks the entire scene from a lofty perch.

The Ladew Gardens are both formal and romantic in tone. Their combination of charm, surprise, and beauty will appeal to young and old alike. (Children will delight in finding and identifying the topiary forms.) The estate also includes an elegant home filled with memorabilia, artifacts, and photographs reflecting Mr. Ladew's active social life and travels.

Information: The Ladew Gardens are located at 3535 Jarrettsville Pike in Monkton. A guided tour is required to visit the house and gardens, though you can wander around on your own in the gardens. Open daily April through October, Monday through Friday from 10:00 A.M. to 4:00 P.M. and Saturday and Sunday from 10:30 A.M. to 5:00 P.M. Call (410) 557–9570 or go to www.ladewgardens .com.

Of similar interest: For another visit to a topiary garden, see Green Animals in Portsmouth, Rhode Island (chapter 23).

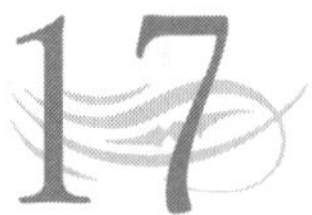

Wethersfield: The Delights of Trompe L'Oeil

Amenia, New York

Directions: From the Taconic State Parkway, take U.S. Highway 44 north of Millbrook, then take County Road 86 (Bangall-Amenia Road). Turn right onto Pugsley Hill Road and follow the signs about 1.3 miles to the entrance on the left.

There are many ways in which gardens can be artistic—or appear to be art themselves. Topiary gardens (see chapters 16 and 23) are like parks of living sculpture, while sculpture parks are themselves gardens of art. In this collection we include gardens designed as Chinese paintings (see chapter 20) and gardens that have been the inspirations for paintings.

At Wethersfield, a country estate near Amenia, New York, you'll find gardens that are at once repositories for sculpture and themselves a kind of spatial work of art. As you walk through the landscaped grounds of Wethersfield, you'll have a sense of trompe l'oeil—that French description of art that plays spatial tricks on the unsuspecting (but delighted) viewer.

Wethersfield's gardens are so artful that the eye can be deceived by the long allées, decorative gates, and the geometric shapes of pruned bushes and trees that form the setting for its marble statuary. The gardens within gardens, the sense of perspective, and the carefully placed statuary reminded us of the surreal gardens of René Magritte's paintings, where a hat may appear over a hedge in a dreamlike green garden of distant proportions and uncertain boundaries.

The gardens are the high point of the visit to this gentleman's country estate (and working farm). There are also tours of a Spanking carriage barn with elegant vehicles of the past, all shined up and ready to go (the owner participated in carriage-driving competitions), and of the large house, which, despite some real art treasures, is not terribly interesting.

If you want to see everything, you must call for an appointment. Upon your (prearranged) arrival you can decide which parts of the estate are of most interest, but you will surely want to explore the gardens (which can be visited separately), even if you skip the carriage barn or the house tour.

Wethersfield was the home of Chauncey Stillman, an investor and philanthropist, who purchased it in 1937. The estate now consists of 1,400 acres. The setting of the house and gardens is magnificent, overlooking a vast panorama of fields and mountains—the Catskills to the west and the Berkshires to the north. The gardens cover more than ten acres of the estate and provide a marvelous place to walk. There are also woodland paths that you can enjoy at your leisure.

The Georgian-type mansion, built in 1940, is in a traditional colonial style. It houses Stillman's collection of antiques, paintings, furniture, and decorative objects. Elaborate and somewhat overwhelming frescoes by the present-day Italian artist Pietro Annigoni cover a number of walls in a sort of neo-Baroque fashion. There are several paintings by better-known artists, including Toulouse-Lautrec, two Cassatts, an Ingres, a Sargent, and a Degas, as well as many less-well-known works.

There is a great mix of styles and attitudes in these interiors, ranging from the owner's rather chummy den, with its embroidered pillows, to a room that functioned as a Catholic shrine to the pope, with a Murillo painting over the mantel. The most startling room is the south wing, a 1973 addition that Stillman called the "Gloriette," which can only be described as eccentric in style and taste. The guide will describe it all.

And now to the gardens. Leave yourself plenty of time to see them, and even to walk through the woods to the Palladian arches at the edge of the field. Pick up a map at the upper parking lot, where you leave your car; you'll find the brochures in a basket between two stone lions.

The gardens, which you will enter here, are generally neoclassical and French in style. They are simultaneously grand and intimate—you might even see occasional peacocks strolling through them. Each garden is separated from the next with hedges or wrought-iron gates. Though there are formal flower beds, it is the geometric design of borders and flagstone paths, reflecting pools, and green walls of hedges that create the special ambience of this place. There are cones, balls, columns, and boulder-shaped topiary designs, as well as gargoyles and cherubs, temples, animal sculptures, and classical figures everywhere, nestling into the greenery and demarcating each individual area.

You'll find a lily pond with sculptured turtles, deer sculptures by John Flannagan, two Pans by an Englishman named Peter Watts, two nymphs and a Hercules of limestone, some charming recumbent sheep, a naiad by the Swedish sculptor Carl Milles gracing a fountain, and a stone stairway leading to a belvedere with a stunning view of the landscape. A Polish artist named Joseph Stachura created many of Wethersfield's sculptures, including the Madonna and other religious works around the grounds. They are representational marble carvings that are graciously placed here and there in shrinelike settings.

All of the sculptures are traditional—this is not a venue for the latest in abstract works. Instead, it is a period setting with a strikingly "modern" sense of space. Like an outdoor gallery the gardens are a form of three-dimensional art, ornamented with sculpture; the emphasis of the landscape design has surely been on form. But this is not to say that there are not charming flower beds and wonderful trees. There are, in fact, perennial gardens, a rose garden, a cutting garden, and many other distinctive sections, tended by an army of gardeners who work year-round.

Information: Wethersfield is located on Pugsley Hill Road in northern Dutchess County. The house, gardens, and carriage house are open Wednesday, Friday, and Saturday, June 1 through September 30; the gardens are open from noon to 5:00 P.M. Advance reservations are required, and an entrance fee is charged. Call (914) 373–8037.

In the vicinity: The beautiful gardens of Innisfree are not far away (see chapter 20).

18

Opus 40: A Bluestone Environment

Woodstock, New York

Directions: From New York City take the New York State Thruway north to the Saugerties exit. Take Route 212 west through Woodstock and follow the signs along the road.

If you have ever visited an abandoned stone quarry, you know what a dramatic and beautiful sight it can be. Perhaps you have made a comment about nature imitating art, for the picturesque quality of light and shadow on stone and water has long been a favorite subject for artists. A visit and walk through Opus 40 will blur the traditional lines of art and nature still further. This abandoned bluestone quarry is an extraordinary example of environmental art in which both art and nature are so intertwined that you will no longer distinguish between them.

Opus 40 is the lifelong enterprise of environmental sculptor Harvey Fite. He bought the six-acre site where bluestone had been quarried and over a thirty-seven-year period transformed it into a monumental environmental sculpture. Fite originally conceived of the abandoned quarry as a dramatic sculpture park for his works, but he found its natural surroundings overpowering for his individual carvings. He removed them to the grassy areas bordering the quarry and set to work to make the quarry itself into his major work of art.

Opus 40 is made up of thousands of tons of stone laid out into pathways, walls, convex and concave shapes, circular formations around quarry springs and trees, and abstract monuments. You can walk through it and around it, climb on it, enjoy different angles and views of nearby Overlook Mountain, and in general lose yourself within this total art environment.

In the center, and at the summit, of Opus 40 you'll find Fite's monolith, a nine-ton stone column from which the patterns of the sculpture radiate. It is here at the center that some visitors choose to sit and meditate, and where jazz and folk music concerts and other events are held on summer afternoons.

In addition to the quarry area, you can also walk on nicely wooded paths around the acreage or loll on the grassy areas where Fite's more traditional sculptures are set. In summer several (non-swimming) pools and fountains that are part of the environmental site are filled with water, making this a pleasant outing on a hot day.

The Quarryman's Museum is also on the property. Fite built it to house his collection of tools and artifacts used by quarrymen and to honor and explain the tradition of quarrying and stonework. Hand-forged folk tools and a slide show on the construction of Opus 40 are among the museum's offerings.

The carefully conceived and rather formalistic patterns of Opus 40 make this one of the more interesting environmental art sites we have visited. Nevertheless, you may wonder—as do many critics of environmental art—whether the natural state of an abandoned quarry is not equally inspiring or aesthetically interesting, with its accidental piles of fallen rock and haphazard design around a central space. Whatever your view, you'll find Fite's transformation of this giant art site extraordinary, and a visit there a rewarding and thought-provoking experience.

Information: Opus 40 is located at 7480 Fite Road in Saugerties. It is open May through October every day except Tuesday from 10:00 A.M. to 4:00 P.M. and Sunday from noon to 5:00 P.M. There is a small admission fee, but children under twelve are admitted free. Group tours are available. Rubber-soled shoes are recommended. Call (845) 246–3400 or visit www.opus40.org.

In the vicinity: Woodstock, the small village nearby, has long been known as an artists' colony (though its name is now linked with the music festival, which actually took place many miles away); it has summer exhibitions and a variety of crafts and studio workshops. Sugar Loaf (see chapter 13), a crafts village, is also not far away, off Route 17.

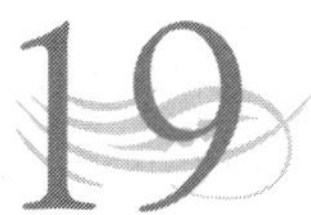

Untermyer Park: The Neoclassical Tradition

Yonkers, New York

Directions: From New York City take the Hutchinson River Parkway north and exit at 250th Street. Go north on Riverdale Avenue, which becomes Warburton Avenue. Take Warburton Avenue into Yonkers, where you come to a small cross street called Odell; turn left. This will bring you to North Broadway (U.S. Highway 9). Turn left on North Broadway, and Untermyer Park will be on your right.

If you are looking for a way to introduce young children to the pleasures of art and architectural discovery outside the confines of a museum, try taking them to Untermyer Park in Yonkers. Here, in a short and delightful walk, they can discover a variety of interesting sculptures, architectural details, and classical-era art without knowing they are being educated at all! If you do this walk in the form of a treasure hunt, they will enjoy it all the more.

Untermyer Park was once the estate of Samuel Untermyer, a well-to-do lawyer who made his home, Greystone, there at the turn of the century. (Greystone was an imposing place where a governor of New York, Samuel J. Tilden, lived from 1874 to 1876.) The house was demolished some time ago, but the 113-acre garden, designed by William Welles Bosworth for Untermyer (an amateur horticulturalist himself) was saved. In 1946 it was donated to the city of Yonkers and, through the efforts of preservationists, the city, and the state with federal funds, is still being restored.

And there is a lot worth saving. In addition to the beautifully landscaped gardens, there is literally a treasure trove of small art details in the neoclassical revival style favored by Bosworth and Untermyer. Perched on a hill with a great Hudson River view to the west, the park is a large rectangle surrounded on the other three sides by a high brick wall, which increases the lovely sense of isolation from the modern noise and confusion of a busy roadway just outside the gates.

The park is a formal arrangement with a central reflecting pool bordered by shrubbery. There are wonderful columns and white walkways that make you think you are strolling among ancient ruins. At the north end of the park is an amphitheater with Ionic columns; at the western side is a circular temple in the classical style overlooking a pool decorated with Roman-style mosaics (perhaps best seen in the park's off-season when the pools are not filled). There are several flower gardens that are also decorated with different ancient ornamentation, as well as an artificially constructed rocky area that is reminiscent of a grotto. In addition to seasonal plantings of flowers (particularly nice, of course, in spring and summer), there are impressive old trees here, including beech, Japanese maple, firs, and spectacular massive oaks.

You might begin your walk, if you want to do it as a treasure hunt, by asking your children (or enthusiastic adults) to search for the following sculptural, architectural, or pictorial treasures at Untermyer Park:

Two sphinxes (mythological creatures that look like crouching lions but have wings)

Head of Hermes, or Mercury (the Greek god Hermes, or Roman god Mercury, the messenger; wears a winged cap to show his speed)

Classical-style temple (a small, round temple, complete with classical columns and ornamental fountains)

Greek-style amphitheater (an outdoor theater ornamented with columns and two sphinx sculptures by Paul Manship)

Roman-style pool (a beautiful pool decorated with multicolored mosaic designs)

Two kinds of vine patterns

A lobster

A crab

A skate fish

A sea lion

A starfish

An octopus

A snail

A redfish

Ionic columns (long, slender Greek columns with an ornamental curling design at the top)

Doric columns (compared to Ionic columns, shorter and more massive and solid)

Columned walkway (leads to the rock garden.)

Ancient gateway (Assyrian-style entranceway that contrasts with the delicate Greek columns opposite)

Wave pattern

Snowflake pattern

Whirlwind pattern

Information: Untermyer Park is located at 945 North Broadway (US 9) in Yonkers. It is open daily year-round from dawn to dusk.

In the vicinity: The Hudson River Museum is only about a mile away. This pleasant museum occupies a restored Victorian house and showcases nineteenth- and twentieth-century American painting, sculpture, and decorative arts, with an emphasis on the Hudson River. It's located at 511 Warburton Avenue, Yonkers; telephone (914) 963–4550.

The Hudson River artist Jasper Cropsey lived and worked nearby in Hastings-on-Hudson (see chapter 24).

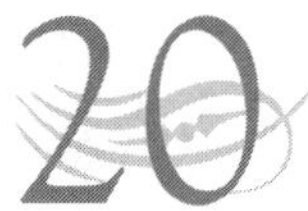

Innisfree Garden: Bringing Chinese Landscape Painting to Life

Millbrook, New York

Directions: From New York City take the Henry Hudson Parkway north to the Saw Mill River Parkway to the Taconic State Parkway; exit at Poughkeepsie/Millbrook (U.S. Highway 44) and go east on US 44. Look for Tyrrel Road on your right; the entrance to Innisfree is from Tyrrel Road.

The artistic gardens of Innisfree are well worth a foray into the countryside. Created in the 1920s to reflect the philosophy and aesthetic of Chinese gardens, they bring you to a world very different from that of most gardens in our region. Experiencing Innisfree means taking an inspiring journey and exploring nature through Chinese artistic tradition. In fact, a walk here is akin to finding a series of Chinese landscape paintings that are real and three-dimensional, and then strolling right into them.

Walter Beck, a painter, and his wife, Marion, spent twenty-five years creating these vast gardens. Their inspiration came primarily from the eighth-century Chinese scrolls of the poet/painter Wang Wei, where scenes in nature are unfolded gradually. The basic design idea of Innisfree is the "cup garden"—a Chinese tradition dating back hundreds of years. The Chinese would set apart an object by "framing" it in such a way that it would be distinct and apart from its surroundings. According to Lester Collins, the landscape architect who has been in charge of Innisfree for many years, "You build a picture out of nature; you control the floor and the walls, and you bring the sky down."

Walking through Innisfree is analogous to walking through an art gallery from one picture to the next—from a meadow to a moss-covered rock to a lotus pool—in each case concentrating on the element before you. As in the case of a work of art, each destination has been carefully created to affect the viewer's senses in a certain way. Nature has been tamed completely, and even though the terrain at Innisfree may look wild and free, nothing has been left to chance. The land has been cleared, and waterfalls, streams, and pools have been created.

"In their gardens," says Collins, "the Chinese express life and death and everything together—the pain and the wonder." The two main elements of Chinese gardens, mountains and rocks (yang) and water (yin), are very important in this garden and provide the necessary counterpoint of life. Yin is passive, dark, and moist; and yang is active, bright, and aggressive. According to the Chinese, a harmonious arrangement of mountains and water can give the viewer a spiritual experience of universal harmony. Water and rocks of all sizes and shapes are everywhere set amid soft foliage, shrubs, and trees. Flowers are not an important element in Chinese gardens, but here you will find delicate clematis growing on an arbor, primroses, forget-me-nots, water irises, and hydrangeas.

Innisfree is a garden for all seasons, since it emphasizes the architecture of its basic elements in harmony with one another. (Note, however, that it is open only May through October.) You can enjoy it under any weather conditions, as a great garden "is good aesthetically and has nothing to do with climate," according to Collins. In fact, on one of our visits we experienced torrential rains. But the downpours only echoed the usual sounds of the nearby streams and waterfalls, and the soft colors of the foliage were rendered the more vivid by the rain.

Before setting out on your walk, pick up a map near the parking lot. A network of paths will take you around the lake (from where you'll see a tantalizing little island of pines that can be explored) and up and down gently sloping hills. Chinese gardens are supposed to be miniatures of nature's way; here, too, you will walk past small evocations of mountains, streams, and forests, experiencing each sensation as a traveler might in the open countryside, or as a viewer who encounters an unfolding Chinese handscroll landscape painting. You'll come across a mist fountain, a rock garden waterfall, a curious "Fu Dog" stone statue, a hillside cave, a brick terrace (where you can rest and take in the view), fantastic rocks in the shapes of turtles and dragons, bird and bat houses, water sculptures, and hemlock woods. Don't fail to look about you at distant views as well.

Information: Innisfree is open May through October on Wednesday, Thursday, and Friday from 10:00 A.M. to 4:00 P.M. and Saturday and Sunday from 11:00 A.M. to 5:00 P.M. Admission is charged. Call (914) 677–8000 or visit www.innisfreegarden.org.

In the vicinity: Nearby Millbrook has an unusually pleasant town park, if you haven't had your fill of nature walking.

Of similar interest: Also in Dutchess County is another exquisite garden, Wethersfield (see chapter 17) in nearby Amenia.

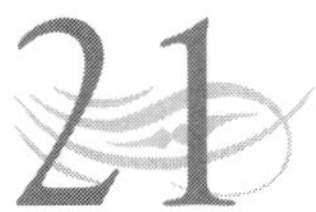

Cedaridge Farm: Impressionist Paintings Brought to Life

Pipersville, Pennsylvania

Directions: Cedaridge Farm is north of Doylestown in eastern Pennsylvania. You will receive specific directions when you make an appointment.

No garden we have seen has made such a conscious (and successful) effort at reproducing an entire era of gardens—and paintings of them—as Derek Fell's Cedaridge Farm. Fell is a photographer and writer with a specialty in gardens and their history. His great interest is the French impressionist and postimpressionist landscape. Using reproductions of some of the most famous paintings by such artists as Monet and van Gogh, he has created living versions of their subjects. At Cedaridge Farm you'll see brightly colored irises under a red arched Japanese-style bridge just as Monet pictured, and a perennial flower border around a vegetable garden as painted by Pissarro. There are fields of flowers as pictured by van Gogh, a leaf tunnel as described by Cézanne, and a jungle garden that captures Rousseau's oversize foliage.

A visit here is, in fact, a very odd experience. For the pure appreciator of pretty and well-designed gardens, it is a large, lovely, and ever-changing landscape. For the art lover who is familiar with the paintings on which each garden tableau is based, it is beautiful but somewhat unnerving. It is like a visit to a famous portrait gallery in which each painted face has come to life.

This is a case of art imitating (and designing) nature and nature, in turn, being used to imitate art. We must remember that the impressionists planted their own gardens with paintings of them in mind. Claude Monet, for example, chose and planted the flowers in his garden at Giverny because he liked their color harmonies, and he actually scattered seeds for tiny white flowers such as baby's breath across the landscape so that he could include their delicate touches in his paintings. Paul Cézanne is known to have cut leaf tunnels through the flowering shrubs in his garden at Aix-en-Provence, giving it a sculptural outlook amid carefully harmonized greens. Pierre-Auguste Renoir, another of Fell's inspirations, created a garden of wildflowers under the olive trees at his home near Nice, relishing the naturalistic look for his paintings. (All of these artists' gardens, by the way, are open to visitors in France.)

Using the impressionists' choice of plantings, color, and design, Fell has chosen to re-create a number of these sites. The flyer and map that you receive when you enter the property takes you from garden to garden. There is a nice, pleasantly informal atmosphere on this self-guided walk; nothing is commercialized or numbered on signs. You can see color reproductions of the paintings in the small house that is used as a gallery and headquarters for visitors. You may look first at the reproductions and then see the gardens, or, as we did, reverse the process. In any case, the verisimilitude is astounding, and we think you will relish following the map whether or not you are there merely to enjoy the pretty settings or are an impressionist painting enthusiast.

You begin your walk through an impressionist meadow of wildflowers and a rose arbor, which will take you to a swamp garden. Next you will find your first garden inspired by a specific artist. Cézanne's Leaf Tunnel is an appealing spot, a study in light and shade created by means of close plantings of bright green Japanese hakone grass and sassafras, scarlet maples, and black walnut trees.

From here you will pass by water lily ponds and a stream garden, visit a Victorian-style conservatory, and enjoy a profusion of flowers in an old-fashioned cottage garden. Soon you will come to Vincent van Gogh's Cutting Garden, a brilliant re-creation of a scene the artist painted in Provence. A gate designed and painted by Gustave Caillebotte (for a Paris garden) is nearby. A moon garden—one of our favorites—features a collection of flowers that are all white or pink so that they will reflect the light of a summer moon.

Next is a perennial-bordered, walled vegetable garden based on Camille Pissarro's unusual design. It includes plants arranged both for color and shape, and a familiar wooden wheelbarrow and several watering cans are artfully displayed. Nearby is a tableau featuring a rope swing like that painted by Renoir.

Henri Rousseau's giant-leaved plants grow in a junglelike setting at the bottom of a sloping hillside. The oversize flora includes umbrella plants, joe-pye weed, plume poppies, and sunflowers. This is a particularly exotic re-creation, since the artist's own paintings were imaginary rather than interpretations of the landscape. (You might find yourself searching for a monkey or a lion amid the foliage.)

The Monet Bridge, with its delightful red arch, is surrounded by and contrasts with brilliant purple irises; it truly makes you feel you have wandered into Giverny by mistake. From here you come upon van Gogh's Woodland Garden, an airy grove of birch trees. A visit to a moss garden and a ramble through the woods bring you back to the visitor center.

These are only a few highlights of Cedaridge Farm. The garden is apparently still being developed; perhaps when you visit, there will be additional settings bringing to mind the shimmering colors and flickering light of the French impressionists and the shapes and forms that inspired the artists who followed them.

Information: Only open to individuals on Memorial Day weekend, Mother's Day weekend, and Father's Day weekend, Friday through Sunday from 10:00 A.M. to 4:00 P.M. Open to groups by appointment on weekdays as well as weekends. As this is a private garden, open weekends are subject to last-minute cancellation. Be sure to get a personal confirmation before you make the drive. Admission is charged. Call (215) 766–2858.

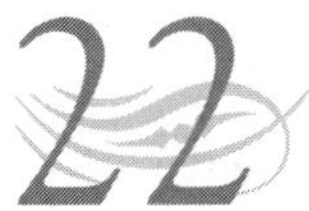

Madoo: An Abstract Expressionist Painter's Garden

Sagaponack, New York

Directions: Take the Long Island Expressway (Interstate 495) to exit 70 to Route 27 east (Montauk Highway). One mile east of the Bridgehampton Village Monument, turn right at the traffic light onto Sagg Main Street and go 1.3 miles; the entrance is on the right.

Madoo is the quintessential artist's garden. It is a vibrant collection of colors and shapes, compositions and patterns. Robert Dash—an abstract expressionist painter, then a landscape realist, and now again an abstractionist—has created a garden that reflects his artistic interests and spontaneity in some forty intersecting and interrelated garden parts. Unlike many designers of great gardens, he believes in the irregular. The overall abundance and ever-changing whimsy of Madoo makes this an original and unlike any garden we have visited.

Madoo (which means "my dove" in Scottish dialect) is a garden without the usual rules. Plants are mixed together with an eye for design and color; decor elements—painted vases, a jauntily posed straw hat, or sudden pieces of brightly colored furniture—are deliberately placed, like bits of still life. Blueberries and roses share one area. Another section is surrounded by high boxwood hedges that enclose a channel for rainwater; nearby is a sod bench like that seen in medieval woodcuts. There is an arched Chinese bridge, a laburnum walk, and abundant privet shrubs pruned to resemble dancers. Each section of the garden can be seen as a fanciful outdoor room with its own decor and visual logic. But these separate garden rooms share boundaries with one another, and from certain vantage points the viewer can see many sections as part of a whole.

Set on almost two acres of windswept land on Long Island's south shore, Madoo is directly next door to a working farm. The contrast between the neighboring long, straight rows of crops and Dash's wildly irregular plantings adds to the visual delight. When the artist bought the property in 1966, it consisted of only some eighteenth-century sheds and a 1740 barn. He has since moved structures and built two studios and two houses; some of the buildings form a low compound creating a sheltered courtyard for part of the garden. Even the weather-beaten, brown shingled buildings became part of the riot of color; the woodwork is now painted violet and chartreuse, apparently to complement the current colors in the garden.

Madoo has evolved over the years into a whimsical and luxurious fantasyland. For the past few years it has been open one day a week in season as a conservancy, but the artist's creative personality (and amiable presence on visiting days) makes a visit here a far cry from touring the usual impersonal and formal conservancy garden.

When you arrive (and pay the rather steep price, but it helps keep the garden going), you are given a map of Madoo. It designates forty areas and tells you how to get from one to the next. There are playful walkways, steps, and bridges if you follow the plan thoroughly.

(One such construction is described as "a stairway to absolutely nowhere.") The map's accompanying description gives some idea of the scope of the artist's range of horticultural interests, from mazes, bird-welcoming plants, and a High Renaissance "view-swiper" perspective path to a fifth-century quincunx bed mentioned by Cyrus the Great.

Many of the plantings were chosen to withstand the heavy gales of the seaside site. Among the numerous flowers to be seen are some three dozen varieties of primroses, rugosa roses, Ship's roses, and several other exotic rose species; Silver Moon clematis; and yellow lilies and mullein. Exotic trees and shrubs include wonderful ginkgo trees, sculpturally pruned lilac and false cypress trees, weeping English oak, taiga birch, native pawpaw, and pollarded willows twisted in the wind. Three small ponds support a variety of grasses and border plants as well as frogs and fishes.

But all is not neatly arranged or described. There is an overall feeling of playful disorder and jungly overgrowth in parts of the property that make a visit here a bit like touring a funhouse in garden form—one section even has mirrors. And the artist's constantly evolving designs ensure that every visit will be different from the one before.

Information: Madoo is located at 618 Sagg Main Street in Sagaponack, not far from East Hampton on Long Island. It is open only during the summer months on Wednesday from 1:00 to 5:00 P.M. Children under six are not permitted, but we recommend the garden for older kids. Admission is charged. Call (516) 537–0802 or visit www.madoo.org.

Green Animals: A Topiary Kingdom Made of Yew

Portsmouth, Rhode Island

Directions: From Providence take Interstate 95 south to the Wyoming exit, then Route 138 east to Newport. At the junction of Routes 138 and 114, take Route 114 and continue for about 7 miles north to Cory's Lane; the entrance to Green Animals is on the left.

If you like animal sculptures prettily set along garden paths—and wish to see some whimsical examples that are neither stone nor steel—make a visit to this topiary garden where growing trees and bushes are trimmed into myriad shapes, both abstract and realistic. Green Animals is a small estate whose gardens are filled with members of the animal kingdom, including a giraffe, a giant camel, a bear, a swan, an elephant, a rooster, and even a unicorn, all made of greenery. Set into a formal garden of flowers and hedges and geometric pathways, these cavorting animals are a particular delight to children.

Green Animals, not far from Newport, overlooks Narragansett Bay and is the oldest topiary garden in the country. The seven-acre estate includes a summer house with original furnishings from its nineteenth-century past and a toy collection, but it is particularly the topiary garden that draws visitors. The garden was the idea of a family named Brayton, who were enchanted by topiary gardens they had seen in the Azores. They and their gardeners, Joseph Carreiro (a native of the Azores) and his son-in-law, George Medonca, designed the garden, beginning their work around 1893.

Green Animals' sculptures, made from nature, are both realistic and fanciful. The garden includes about one hundred pieces of topiary art, including geometric shapes, arches and ornamental designs, and some twenty-one animals and birds. The topiary works are made from yew and privet. Other specialties of the garden are thirty-five seasonally planted flower beds in the most perfect condition. There are peach trees and fig trees, grape arbors, and various other horticultural pleasures.

In pleasant weather children can sit on tiny animal-shaped rocking chairs out among the topiary fantasies. Green Animals is included in a combination ticket with several Newport mansions or can be visited separately (at what we thought was unfortunately a rather steep price). If you would enjoy visiting Newport's great houses with their elegant period furnishings and art, however, the combination ticket is well worth the cost.

Information: Green Animals (401–683–1267) is on Cory's Lane in Portsmouth. It is open daily May to mid-November from 10:00 A.M. to 5:00 P.M. Admission is charged.

In the vicinity: The great mansions of Newport are not far away. These glamorous, art-filled reminders of the gilded era are filled with art and artifacts, and many are open to the public. For information on the combined ticket with Green Animals, call the Preservation Society of Newport County at (401) 847–1000.

Gilbert Stuart's birthplace in Saunderstown, Rhode Island (815 Gilbert Stuart Road; 401–294–3001), is a charming eighteenth-century snuff mill with a waterwheel. Though there are no original Stuart portraits here, you'll find a nice atmosphere and interesting colonial displays, including material on Stuart's career as a painter.

Of similar interest: Another major topiary garden, Ladew Topiary Gardens in Monkton Maryland, is described in chapter 16.

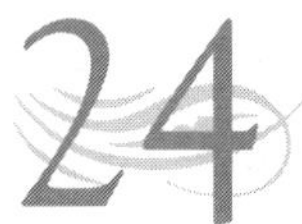

A Lower Hudson River Valley Art Tour

Hastings-on-Hudson to Beacon, New York

Directions: To reach the Cropsey house from New York City, take the Henry Hudson Parkway north (it becomes the Saw Mill River Parkway). Exit left at the Hastings sign and continue on Main Street to the village of Hastings-on-Hudson. At the intersection of Main Street and Warburton Avenue, turn left and go 1 block to Washington Avenue, where you make another left. The Cropsey house and studio will be on your left. For Kykuit: Take Route 9 north to the visitor center at Philipsburg Manor in Tarrytown; a van will take you to the estate. To continue to Union Church from Tarrytown: Turn right onto Route 448 and follow the winding road to Pocantico Hills. The church is on the right. For Manitoga: From Route 9 find Route 9D, which runs parallel but closer to the river, and continue north. You'll find Manitoga on your right, about 2 miles south of the town of Garrison.

This area of the Hudson River Valley is still—a century after its fame as the subject of the first major landscape movement in the nation—home to numerous art sites. On this outing we take you to the delightful home and studio of one of those Hudson River painters, Jasper Cropsey; then north a short distance to see the spectacular art collection of the Rockefeller family at Kykuit; followed by a small church with windows by Chagall and Matisse just down the road; and finally to the unbelievably scenic home and studio of the designer Russel Wright at Manitoga near Garrison. If you are feeling energetic, you can combine these sites with additional ones: not far away are Untermyer Park (see chapter 19) and, on the other side of the river, Storm King (see chapter 40).

We begin with Cropsey. Visiting a nineteenth-century artist's home and studio is one of the pleasures that are all too rare today. Most have been updated and changed beyond recognition; in some cases the artist lived so frugally that there was not much to see and the house is long gone. However, one such artist's home and studio attests to the care and interest of the painter's great-granddaughter, who saved, polished, and otherwise re-created the wonderful Victorian atmosphere in which American painter Jasper Cropsey lived in his pretty yellow house in Hastings-on-Hudson. You can visit this beautiful home and its grand artist-designed studio by appointment, and we found such a visit delightful.

Cropsey lived here from 1885 until his death in 1900, and his descendants continued to occupy the house until they made it a museum in the late 1970s. Cropsey obviously had a fine eye for design and architecture, as well as Hudson River school landscape painting. You will see numerous examples of his oils, prints, and wonderful line drawings in his home, including many views of the surrounding countryside—from Hudson River vistas to the small communities that border its banks.

There are portraits, clothing (several of his wife's elegant dresses are on display), his palette and paints, a desk he designed, and numerous other items that give a real feel of the artist's household and the era itself. The high point (literally) is the many-storied studio with an elaborate system of pulleys to bring in fresh air, all paneled in polished fruitwood and designed by the artist. In fact, Cropsey was apparently one of those ingenious nineteenth-century Americans who did many things well: He did not restrict himself to painting his well-observed, realistic landscape views; he also designed buildings—including two churches—and a variety of imaginative interior details for his house and studio.

Your second stop is Kykuit (the name means "lookout" in Dutch), a grand, early twentieth-century American villa magnificently situated with sweeping views of the Hudson. It includes the imposing mansion, complete with its impressive art collection and antiques, as well as the spectacular gardens filled with first-rate sculptures.

On the two-hour tour you are told about the genesis of the estate—surprisingly modest in its earliest version—and its evolution with succeeding generations of Rockefellers; about the lifestyle of the family and its impact on the configuration of the house; and about the provenance of the many artworks and objects. The gardens were originally designed by the landscape architect William Welles Bosworth, a personal friend of John D. Rockefeller Jr.; subsequent additions were supervised by Abby Rockefeller, a dedicated gardener in her own right.

The most impressive addition to the outdoor spaces is the superb collection of modern sculptures, acquired and placed by Nelson Rockefeller. After having given away much of his art to major museums, he left some seventy important and large outdoor sculptures here. As you wander around the lovely terraces and gardens, you can enjoy the works of most of the twentieth century's masters, ranging from Matisse and Nadelman to Moore and Giacometti. The sculptures have been carefully placed to enhance each piece as well as the surrounding ornamental gardens, lawns, or walls. Most have been left exactly where Rockefeller placed them, even in such unlikely places as the golf course. The majority are situated in the formal gardens next to the house. You will probably wish for more time to linger in these glorious sculpture gardens that combine the best in contemporary art and landscape design.

Leaving Kykuit, head to the tiny, charming, ivy-covered Union Church in nearby Pocantico Hills. Here you will see a rare treat for this country: a series of stained-glass windows by Marc Chagall and Henri Matisse that are brilliant in color and glorious in this modest country church. The rose window is by Matisse, while the cycle of nine windows by Chagall is the only such series the artist ever produced. Seven are devoted to Old Testament prophets. This is a rare treat—don't miss it!

Heading north again, you'll come to the spectacular woodland quarry site called Manitoga, the Russel Wright Design Center. The industrial designer's home and studio, known as Dragon Rock, are built on the very edge of a dramatic rocky cliff overlooking an abandoned quarry. Waterfalls and falling rock make this as beautiful a setting as any artist could ask for. You can hike through 75 acres of designed (but very rustic) landscape on 4 miles of woodland paths. Tours of the modern house and studio are offered daily (in the morning) from April to October, but you must phone for a reservation. For three decades after he purchased the land and abandoned quarry in 1942, Wright, a committed naturalist, masterfully designed the landscape and a house to complement it. He had a love of natural shapes, which can be seen both outside (in the carefully placed stones and log bridge) and inside the house.

In this, the only twentieth-century modern home open to the public in New York State, you will see examples of industrial and domestic design that Wright pioneered. "Good design is for everyone," he maintained, and his furniture, pottery, and glassware are a testament to his fascination with organic shapes and materials. When you arrive, take the self-guided walking trail (at the parking area), which will not only guide you through the pathways, but will also explain Wright's philosophy.

Information: The Cropsey house and studio are located at 49 Washington Avenue, Hastings-on-Hudson, and can be visited by appointment only Monday through Friday from 10:00 A.M. to 1:00 P.M.; call (914) 478–1372. Admission is charged.

You must make also an appointment to visit Kykuit; tours begin at the visitor center at Philipsburg Manor in Tarrytown (from there you will be taken by minivan to Kykuit). Open daily, except Tuesday, May through November; admission is charged. Call (914) 631–9491 or go to www.hudsonvalley.org.

Union Church is on Route 448 in Pocantico Hills. It is open year-round every day from 10:00 A.M. to 4:00 P.M. Call (914) 631–8200 or visit www.hudsonvalley.org.

Manitoga/The Russel Wright Center is on Route 9D in Garrison. House tours are given daily in the morning April through October. Admission is charged. Call (845) 424–3812 or go to www.russelwrightcenter.org.

In the vicinity: Not far away are the Storm King Art Center (see chapter 40) and Untermyer Park (see chapter 19).

Near the Cropsey house and also in Hastings-on-Hudson, at 25 Cropsey Lane, you'll find the Newington Cropsey Foundation Gallery of Art. This elegant octagonal gallery houses the largest collection of Cropsey's art. Call (914) 478–7990 for hours open or for an appointment.

Master Painters and Sculptors of the Past: Artists' Homes and Ateliers

An Impressionists' Boardinghouse

Old Lyme, Connecticut

Directions: From New Haven take Interstate 95 north to exit 70; go left at the end of the ramp, turn right at the light, then take a left at the intersection with U.S. Highway 1. The museum is the second building on the left.

"Old Lyme was found by many of our masters in landscape to possess remarkable advantages in its great variety, which ranges from the low land of estuaries and salt meadows to the rugged, romantic beauty of rolling glacial hills . . . the village is one of the oldest in New England and is one of the few remaining places which still possess the characteristics expressive of the quiet dignity of other days."

So rhapsodized the painter Frank Vincent DuMond in 1903, in describing the charms of Old Lyme, Connecticut, and its environs—an area to which he and many of his contemporaries first went to live and paint around the turn of the last century. Soon Old Lyme became one of the most famous art colonies in the country. Today, anyone who walks along the village's unspoiled tree-lined streets, leafy lanes, and romantic riverbanks can still appreciate what so captivated these artists.

Old Lyme's enchanting natural setting—with its network of waterways surrounding the Connecticut River and Long Island Sound, and its soft, impressionistic countryside of salt meadows, lowland estuaries, and open fields—along with its brilliant summer light, made it a paradise for painters. As Henry Ward Ranger, the most prominent of the colony's early artists, said, "It looks like Barbizon, the land of Millet . . . it is only waiting to be painted." Here, like the Barbizon school in France, landscapists were to paint out of doors, "en plein air," to catch firsthand the impression or essence of their natural surroundings.

The painter Clark Voorhees (who first explored the area on bicycle, a much recommended way even today) encouraged Ranger to come to Old Lyme in 1899. He took his room and board at the then somewhat dilapidated, but still gracious, Georgian mansion of Miss Florence Griswold, an enterprising, energetic, and committed art lover whose personal fortunes had come upon hard times. Her boardinghouse, the Florence Griswold House (today an elegant museum housing many important works and memorabilia of the Lyme artists), became the home of the art colony, and Miss Florence (as she was affectionately called), its muse.

This cheerful and accommodating lady did everything she could to make the artists feel at home. She encouraged their creativity by providing an environment of intellectual stimulation, camaraderie, and good spirits. Her property included some eleven acres of meadows and orchards abutting the Lieutenant River, where artists could wander around and paint at will. Scattered about were a number of outbuildings that could function as studios, making the entire setup ideal for an art colony. And so it flourished, mainly as a summer place for artists dedicated to living in tune with nature's cycles and capturing on canvas the lovely landscape.

In addition to Ranger, at first the "American Barbizon" included such "tonalists" as Lewis Cohen, Alphonse Jongers, and Henry Rankin Poore, among others. In 1903 its artistic clientele changed upon the arrival of the already well regarded and peripatetic Childe Hassam and his fellow impressionists.

Hassam had come to Old Lyme after having traveled abroad and up and down the New England coastline, painting as he went, always searching for new, unspoiled seaside locales to capture on canvas. He found this area quite similar to that around the farm of his like-minded painter friend J. Alden Weir in Ridgefield, Connecticut (see chapter 29), and was immediately drawn to it. With him came such artists as Willard Metcalf, Walter Griffin, Edward Simmons, Edward Rook, William Chadwick, and Bessie Vonnoh—all friends of Hassam's and followers of the impressionist style. Unlike the tonalists, who captured the tranquility of nature in muted color harmonies, these artists played upon the bright summer light and used intense color schemes in their work. Many of them had studied in France and had been inspired by Claude Monet, Alfred Sisley, and others who were several years ahead of them, but their work had a distinctive American stamp and a greater fascination with the factual.

Impressionism had already been launched in the late nineteenth century in this country by such influential painters as Weir, John Twachtman, and William Merritt Chase, all of whom taught at the Art Students League in New York City. But it was at Old Lyme that the movement coalesced and became so influential, largely due to the energy and work of Hassam. Clearly the leader among his peers at the art colony, he became a great favorite of Miss Florence's and was given the most desirable studio on the grounds—facing the Lieutenant River. Here he painted many of his most famous works, among them *Late Afternoon (Sunset)*, which portrays the river in softly dimming crepuscular light. This theme particularly inspired Hassam, who was intrigued by the poetic effects of light over water. (You can see this painting, and the two mentioned below, at the Griswold Museum.)

The Griswold mansion itself became a popular subject to paint. Will Howe Foote's *Summer Night* (1906) shows a dreamy moonlit view of the facade of the house. He had clearly been inspired by his colleague Willard Metcalf, who just a few months before had painted *May Night*, which won a grand prize at the Corcoran Gallery of Art and became the most celebrated of the Old Lyme paintings. William Chadwick's *On the Porch* (1908, Griswold Museum) depicts the outdoor dining room on the mansion's veranda, where the artists enjoyed eating and conversing alfresco. A seated female figure (probably Chadwick's wife, Pauline) is shown savoring the last remnants of a meal after her luncheon companions have adjourned, probably to rest or paint. In a typical impressionistic mode, the essence of the scene is captured through color, texture, and play of light within a natural setting.

After Monet began painting at his idyllic country estate at Giverny in northern France, it became a center for the impressionist movement. Americans, eager to follow the new directions in French painting, sought a "Giverny of America" where they too could paint outdoors and explore the impressionist style in views of local subjects. Old Lyme became their "Giverny." They created colorful canvases such as Matilda Browne's *Clark Voorhees House* (1905) and Edmund W. Greacen's *The Old Garden* (1912), both of which are in the Griswold Museum collection. They painted local trees—especially the stately elms, oaks, and chestnuts that enhanced the countryside—as in Voorhees's *Winter Landscape*, and the meandering rivers and streams. Popular sites included the Bow Bridge over the Lieutenant River, quite near the Griswold mansion. This picturesque bridge—alas, long since gone—can be seen in Hassam's painting *Bridge at Old Lyme* (Georgia Museum of Art, University of Georgia). It evokes a bygone era of quiet pleasures in a peaceful setting.

A favorite theme of Hassam's was the First Congregational Church, a stately colonial landmark, which he depicted many times, much as Monet had painted several versions of the Bourges Cathedral under different conditions of light. The church, with its tall spire towering above the village's clapboard houses and winding lanes, was to Hassam quintessentially New England in its spirit. The pediment is supported by four Ionic columns topped by a square clock tower; above that, a spire is ornamented by a finial. (You can see Hassam's works picturing this church at the Corcoran Gallery of Art in Washington D.C., and the Smith College Museum of Art in Northampton, Massachusetts.) The church burned down in 1907 but was immediately rebuilt to replicate the original; it can be visited on this outing.

The paintings that were produced at Old Lyme were usually exhibited in the town library at the end of the summer season, until the artists finally formed the Lyme Art Association in 1914 to raise money and build their own gallery right next to the Griswold House. (It became the first self-financed art gallery built by a summer art colony.) It was among the most highly acclaimed art colonies in America during the teens and attracted to its exhibits many collectors, dealers, and art enthusiasts. The colony continued to thrive well into the 1920s, but by the 1930s, with the strong currents of modern art, Old Lyme became more of a historic site than an active art colony.

The Florence Griswold Museum was officially opened in 1947 and joined in 1955 with the Lyme Historical Society to form an organization dedicated to furthering the public's awareness and appreciation of the Lyme artists. To gain a fuller understanding of the artists and their lifestyles and times, we recommend that you visit the museum and then explore the village and countryside that so inspired them. A walk around Old Lyme is pleasant in all seasons, though you might prefer visiting during the spring and summer months, when the artists mostly worked here and the landscape is green and inviting.

Begin at the Florence Griswold Museum on Lyme Street, where you can easily park your car. The gracious, immaculately kept Georgian mansion was designed by Samuel Belcher (the architect of the First Congregational Church of Old Lyme) and is considered an important landmark. The museum contains more than 900 paintings, drawings, watercolors, and prints by some 130 American artists, most of whom were members of the colony. (Obviously the collection is not on display in its entirety.) For history buffs there are thousands of documents relating to the colony, as well as amusing photographs showing the artists' life here. You'll see them enjoying a jolly summer lunch on the porch (there seemed to have been quite a number of bons vivants among this group!), or engrossed in a painting class out of doors, or on a horse-drawn wagon en route to a beach picnic.

The centerpiece of the museum is Miss Florence's famous dining room, the site of many bountiful feasts, still kept much as it was during the heyday of the colony. On the walls and doors is a unique collection of panels painted by the artists as a special gift to her. (Apparently she had adopted a somewhat laissez-faire attitude when it came to financial arrangements with her artists, for which they were most grateful.) The museum organizes temporary exhibitions to illuminate certain features in the permanent collection.

Recent exhibitions have included *Notable Women of Lyme*, *A Summer Day* (focusing on Old Lyme as a summer resort with related paintings, photos, and memorabilia), and *Old Lyme: The American Barbizon*. You might enjoy walking around the grounds surrounding the museum, although they are much reduced from the eleven acres of Miss Florence's time.

On your walk, bike ride, or walk/car ride (depending on your inclination) through the village, you will pass several spots that recall the halcyon days of the colony—from some of the artists' homes (now private) to sites they painted. (Some artists bought their own homes after discovering Miss Florence's inn.) Just two doors to the right of the museum (as you face the entrance) is the former home of Edward Rook (now private), and to the left of the museum is the Lyme Art Association, which continues to have group shows and is open to the public.

If you continue your walk past the Art Association on Lyme Street, you'll come to the main street in the historic district. You will walk past antique, well-preserved clapboard houses with charming old-fashioned flower gardens and fine old trees. After about 0.5 mile you will come to a little side street on your right, Beckwith Lane. Go down the lane to the end and turn right onto Lieutenant River Lane (it may not be identified, but you can't miss it). You will see a small parking area for cars and behind it a grassy path leading to a small dock right on the Lieutenant River, one of the few public accesses to this often painted site. The narrow meandering river surrounded by tall reeds and marshes is a rare and peaceful spot and as unspoiled as it must have been when Miss Florence's artists worked at this site. (You would find it hard to equal this idyllic spot for a picnic.)

Retrace your steps back to Lieutenant River Lane and go a few feet in the other direction for your second view of the river at another small public access. Return to the lane, and continue to Ferry Road. This small intersection is the original site of the Old Lyme Inn, where some of the artists, their friends, and patrons occasionally stayed. (Today's Old Lyme Inn is on Lyme Street, across the street from the museum.) Turn left on Ferry Road to the Congregational Church. This fine reconstruction of the famous 1817 structure is totally convincing, and it's a key spot in the village. Walk back to the museum along Lyme Street, just under a mile's trek. (If you don't wish to make this long loop on foot starting and ending at the museum, you can drive to the Town Hall on Lyme Street, park in the lot behind it and walk from there.)

Information: The Florence Griswold Museum is located at 96 Lyme Street. It is open Tuesday through Saturday from 10:00 A.M. to 5:00 P.M. and Sunday from 1:00 to 5:00 P.M. Call (860) 434–5542 or go to www.flogris.org.

Of similar interest: Two other Connecticut sites for American impressionists are Weir Farm (see chapter 29) and the Bush-Holley House in Cos Cob. The Bush-Holley House and the waterfront in this village were at the center of Cos Cob's days as an art colony around the turn of the twentieth century. As many as 200 artists worked in Cos Cob, beginning with the impressionist John Henry Twachtman, who, with his close friend J. Alden Weir, began painting there in about 1890. Two generations of painters, ranging from the first American impressionists to the early abstractionists who helped organize the Armory Show in 1913, made Cos Cob a mecca for artists.

Twachtman and other artists and writers gathered at the Holley family boardinghouse, where room and board ran about $8.00 per week. You can visit the house, now a museum, at 39 Strickland Road; telephone (203) 622–9686. Like Old Lyme, Cos Cob was the setting for dozens of landscape paintings. A Sunday walking tour will take you to some of the painters' favorite sites, including the many clapboard houses that led Childe Hassam to describe the colony as "the Cos Cob Clapboard School of Art." Call the Greenwich Library Information Center at (203) 622–7910 for details.

Chesterwood: The Home and Studio of Daniel Chester French

Stockbridge, Massachusetts

Directions: From Boston take Interstate 90 (the Massachusetts Turnpike) west to exit 2, then take Route 102 west to its junction with Route 183. Turn left onto Route 183 for 1 mile to a fork in the road. Turn right onto a blacktop road, travel a few yards, and turn left. Continue 0.5 mile to Chesterwood.

The lovely region of western Massachusetts known as "The Berkshires" is endowed with charming vistas, mountains, rivers, lakes, and little New England villages. The area has long attracted seekers of unspoiled natural beauty, including many artists and writers. Daniel Chester French, the famed neoclassical sculptor of monumental works, came to establish a summer home and studio in the shadow of Monument Mountain near Stockbridge. When you visit Chesterwood, his remarkable country estate, you will come away feeling that he could not have chosen a more idyllic spot. He was an artist who really knew how to live.

French became the nation's leading classical sculptor in the early decades of the twentieth century. After studying the Beaux-Arts style in Paris in the late 1880s, he returned to America to establish his own studio. He began his illustrious career making allegorical figures that represented the lofty civic and patriotic aims of the nation. Along with Augustus Saint-Gaudens, he produced many of the most important neoclassical statues at major sites all over the country. Among his colossal allegorical female figures are the sculptures titled *The Republic* (a commission of the World's Columbia Exposition in Chicago in 1893) and the *Four Continents* (at the New York Custom House, now the home of the National Museum of the American Indian).

Later works combined portraiture with personification. Giant figures that were both lifelike and monumental brought French increasing fame and public commissions, among them his most famous work, the Lincoln Memorial statue in Washington D.C., (you will see the various working versions of this statue at Chesterwood). His ability to create heroic, allegorical figures in a naturalistic style was well suited to the taste of the nation, and even after the advent of modernism, he continued to receive honors and awards.

At the height of his career, internationally known and able to live in grand style, French decided to create a perfect working and living environment in the country for himself and his family (although he continued to maintain a winter studio in New York City). He and his wife first saw the rustic farm that was to become Chesterwood while on a horse-drawn carriage trip through the Housatonic River Valley in 1896.

Beautifully situated on a rural road, the 150-acre property—now a museum operated by the National Trust for Historic Preservation—would become the Frenches' summer home for the next thirty-three years. It was at Chesterwood—amid the enchantment of romantic gardens, lawns, and woodlands—that French was inspired to create many of his most important works, including the Lincoln Memorial statue; the *Minute Man* for Concord, Massachusetts; and the *Alma Mater* for Columbia University in New York City.

Chesterwood itself became a lifelong project for the sculptor. He carefully fashioned the estate to provide an ideal ambience for his creative needs, as well as for the many brilliant social gatherings he was fond of hosting for his prominent neighbors and friends. (Edith Wharton came regularly from her nearby estate.) The main house and studio, overlooking majestic Monument Mountain, were designed by his architect friend Henry Bacon, but it was French himself who laid out the garden and woodland walks.

To him gardens were like sculptures: A basic design had to be drawn up in order for them to work as art. He planned a central courtyard, an Italianate garden with a graceful fountain, and English flower gardens. Beyond the formal areas he arranged a network of paths leading into and through the hemlock forest, where the walker could enjoy peaceful views. He enjoyed creating aesthetic effects that influenced the quality of daily life. For example, he built a berm (a small artificial hill) along the road leading to the house so that the wheels of approaching carriages could not be seen, causing the carriages to appear to "float" by.

French spent a great deal of time in his garden, from which he derived much of his inspiration. He regularly studied the effects of light and shadow on sculptures that were destined to be out of doors. French found an ingenious way to move these massive works from his studio to the outside. He would place them on a revolving modeling table set on a short railroad track and roll them out into the sunlight, where he could test them in the natural light. You can still see this unusual contraption when you visit the studio.

French and his wife lived and thrived at Chesterwood with their daughter, Margaret French Cresson, also a sculptor. In 1969 the property was donated to the National Trust and converted into the museum you see today.

When you arrive at Chesterwood, you are struck by the beauty of the site: With spectacular mountain views on all sides, it is little wonder French and his family wanted to be here. The house and landscaping are tasteful and harmonious in every sense; there is nothing pretentious or ostentatious about this estate. As the artist once remarked, "I live here six months of the year—in heaven. The other six months I live, well, in New York."

In order to visit the house and studio, you must take an organized tour—about forty-five minutes of fairly detailed information (more than you might want to hear), including a great deal about the social life of the French family and the mores of the time. However, you are free to roam the grounds and woods at will, and can do so at no cost. After you have purchased your tickets for the house and studio, you will probably be directed to the barn to begin the tour. This rustic building, originally part of the working farm that French purchased, has been remodeled into an exhibition gallery. You can wander about and look at the vintage photographs and works by Margaret French Cresson, Augustus Saint-Gaudens, and others.

Aside from the gardens, the studio visit is by far the most satisfying part of the tour. The beautifully designed 22-foot-high structure provided the perfect airy and spacious working environment. It is kept much as it was during French's time, with materials, notebooks, tools, and sketches on view. You'll see plaster cast models and preliminary sculptures of some of his most important works, notably his seated Lincoln (of which there are several versions) and his graceful Andromeda. You'll also see the massive 30-foot double doors that were constructed to accommodate French's many large works; they were built when he first made his impressive equestrian statue of George Washington, now located in the Place d'Iena in Paris. Off to the side of the studio is a cozy room with a couch, piano, and corner fireplace where French entertained. Apparently he enjoyed having friends around even when he worked. In back of the studio is a wide veranda (which he called a "piazza"), with wisteria vines and fine views, and the rail tracks on which his massive sculptures rolled away.

The thirty-room colonial revival house (built in 1900) is nearby. Its gracious rooms, wide hallways, and appealing surroundings are what you would expect from a man of French's refined tastes. Surrounding the house are the charming gardens that French carefully planned and so enjoyed. Take a stroll in them and beyond, on the pine-laden woodsy paths in the forest.

Information: Chesterwood (413–298–3579; www.chesterwood.org) is about 2 miles west of Stockbridge and is open daily May through October from 10:00 A.M. to 5:00 P.M. It is recommended you phone first to check on the schedule. Admission is charged.

In the vicinity: Hancock Shaker Village (413–443–0188), at the junction of U.S. Highway 20 and Route 41 in Pittsfield, was a Shaker community that had its peak in the 1830s. This collection of simple houses and community buildings—including a round stone barn—is an architectural pleasure. You can also watch crafts being made in traditional Shaker style.

The Morris School (431–637–5570) is located on West Street in Lenox. George L. K. Morris and his wife,

Suzy Frelinghuysen, were leading American abstractionists in the 1930s and '40s. They built the first modern house in the entire area, and it became a meeting place for artists (both American and French). The school, which adjoins the original property, boasts a three-paneled outdoor mosaic by Morris, which you may drive onto the grounds to see.

The Mount, also in Lenox, was Edith Wharton's Gilded Age mansion and summer "retreat." Now a certified landmark with tours, resident theater company, and so on, it is quite a tourist attraction. But if you enjoy gardens and interior decoration of the period, or are familiar with Wharton's influential books *The Decoration of Houses* and *Italian Villas and Their Gardens*, it's a "must see," for she based the design of the imposing house and extensive gardens on her own precepts. The Mount is located on Plunkett Street at the junction of Routes 7 and 7A; call (413) 637–1899.

On Shunpike Road in Sheffield, a sculptor named Robert Butler has turned his hilltop grounds with a panoramic view of the Berkshires into the Butler Sculpture Park (413–229–8924). His works are contemporary and abstract, and visitors are welcome.

Of similar interest: For a visit to the home and studio of a contemporary of Daniel Chester French, see Aspet, the Augustus Saint-Gaudens estate (chapter 28). In Peace Dale, Rhode Island, on route 108 near the center of town, you can see an unusually fine example of a Daniel Chester French bronze relief, an allegory called *The Weaver*.

The Thomas Cole House and Frederick Church's Olana

Catskill and Hudson, New York

Directions: To get to the Cole House from New York City, take the New York State Thruway to exit 21 in Catskill, then Route 23 east to the traffic light at Route 385. Turn right and go about 50 feet to the entrance of the Cole House on the left. To reach Olana from the Cole House, take Route 385 to Route 23, turn right, and cross the Rip Van Winkle Bridge (where you should note the extraordinary views). Turn right on Route 9G for 1 mile, following the signs, and wind your way up the hill to Olana.

The Hudson River painters—the American Romantics who glorified nature on canvas in the mid-nineteenth century—drew much of their inspiration from the Hudson Valley, where many of them lived and worked. Thomas Cole, known as the "father" of this school of painting, and Frederick Edwin Church, his illustrious pupil, both lived here. This outing takes you to their homes, which are located on opposite sides of the river, just minutes—but light-years—apart.

The Cole House, an unpretentious white clapboard structure, was the residence of Thomas Cole. Olana, the grand Persian–

style villa dramatically perched atop a hill overlooking the Hudson, was the home of Frederick Church. The Cole House is as modestly understated as Olana is wildly extravagant: While the former is an ordinary early nineteenth-century American farmhouse, the latter is the result of an imagination fueled by the aesthetic fantasies of exotic lands. The contrast between them could not be greater—in architectural style and ambience—yet each provided an inspiring setting for the creation of important works of art.

Thomas Cole moved to his farmhouse in the village of Catskill, located 115 miles north of New York City on the west bank of the Hudson, in 1836. His desire was to live and paint in this glorious spot with its views of the river and the Catskill Mountains. (These views are now partially obscured by overgrown trees on the property.) As he grandly stated, "The Hudson for nature magnificence is unsurpassed . . . The lofty Catskills stand afar—the green hills gently rising from the flood, recede like steps by which we may ascend to a great temple, whose pillars are those everlasting hills, and whose dome is the boundless vault of heaven."

While living here he painted some of his great Catskill landscapes (see chapter 5). His pictures are odes to nature, with their unusual sensitivity to its nuances and intensity, its lights and shadows. He was able to nurture his mystical need to commune with nature in these environs, without having to go far afield. "To walk with nature as a poet is the necessary condition of a perfect artist," he wrote. As Cole was concerned with spiritual and aesthetic—rather than material—values, it is not surprising that he was not a commercially successful artist. His home reflects his simple lifestyle and tastes.

The Cole House remains much like it was, except for the overgrown vegetation on its three-and-a-half-acre property. The small foundation that now operates it has tried to keep the place as

Cole knew it, without giving it the new gloss of a facelift. (You might think that it could use a coat of paint here and there!) Because most of Cole's furniture and personal belongings were sold some years ago, the interior of the house is now quite bare, and you will find few personal mementos. But a visit to this quiet and refreshingly noncommercial spot will give you a sense of who Cole was as an artist and person. You will most likely be able to enjoy the place by yourself, as there are few visitors and no guided tours.

To reach Olana you travel only 3 miles but enter another world. A spacious 250-acre park surrounds the sixteen-room villa, which is often crowded with tourists. The approach to the house is itself on a grand scale, with a network of roads winding up the hill. The house is at the top, with commanding views that Frederick Church captured so beautifully in several of his paintings.

Church was first introduced to the Catskills, "Nature's great Academy of landscape art," in 1844, when he came to study with Thomas Cole, but it was not until fourteen years later that he decided to live here. By then he had become an international celebrity, having traveled throughout the Americas, from Ecuador to Labrador, as well as in Europe and Asia, to experience firsthand natural wilderness at its most elemental. He had created showpiece landscapes that literally galvanized the public, who flocked to see them. His *Niagara* (Corcoran Gallery of Art) was hung by itself; it was so popular it could only be viewed by ticket holders. His *Heart of the Andes* (Metropolitan Museum of Art), a massive 5½-by-10-foot canvas that became one of the most celebrated American paintings of the nineteenth century, was actually preached about in pulpits, where ministers extolled Nature's glories. It would have been unlikely for Church, with his flamboyant style, to have gone off to paint in a quiet spot, as Cole did.

After marrying in 1860, he bought a 126-acre farm south of the town of Hudson, intending, in fact, to live a quiet, rural family life. But with time he inevitably thought in grander terms and acquired more land. Seeing himself as landscape designer in addition to painter, he began to convert the property into a Romantic landscape garden; he created reflecting ponds, planted thousands of trees and many flower gardens, and constructed carriage roads that were carefully placed to enhance a sequence of views. He also decided to build a larger house. What began as plans for a French chateau changed dramatically when Church returned from a trip to the Middle East, enthralled with Moorish architecture. The architect Calvin Vaux (the codesigner of Central Park with Frederick Law Olmsted) was engaged to design something exotic, but it was Church himself who ultimately created Olana ("our place on high" in Arabic).

Church made sketch after sketch, followed by elaborate drawings (much as if he were conceiving a large painting), and he became involved in every detail of the house—from the colors, shapes, and sizes of the rooms; to the placement of windows to frame river views; to the interior decor; to the colorful stencils inside and out. He further enhanced the surrounding gardens to complement the house, adding lookout points where views could be captured. Olana became much more than a place to live; to Church, it became a work of art.

You can appreciate Olana as Church's personal creation when you visit the house and surrounding grounds. A forty-five-minute conducted tour leads you through the house, now a museum, where you enter the private world of the artist. In contrast to the Cole House, Olana is filled with artifacts and objects from years of travel, vintage furniture, works of art, and memorabilia that vividly recall Church's rich and fulfilling cultural and family life. But perhaps the best way to understand Church's art is to wander around the vast property, which you can do on your own, and enjoy the naturalistic gardens and breathtaking views that so inspired him.

Before you begin your walk, pick up a guide to the landscape (available at the ticket office). A map indicates points of interest, including the site of the studio where Church first painted. (He later designed and built a new studio wing onto the main house.) It was probably from this spot that he captured the views immortalized in such landscapes as *The Catskills from Olana* (this painting is located on-site).

Information: The Cole House is open Wednesday through Saturday from 11:00 A.M. to 4:00 P.M. and Sunday 1:00 to 5:00 P.M. during the summer season. There is no admission fee. Call (518) 943–6533.

The grounds of Olana are open daily year-round from 8:30 A.M. to sunset. You will find joggers, walkers, and picnickers enjoying the surroundings. The museum is open April 15 through October 31 by guided tour only, Wednesday through Saturday from 10:00 A.M. to 5:00 P.M. and Sunday noon to 5:00 P.M. (The last tour begins at 4:00 p.m.) Tours are limited to twelve people, so reservations are recommended, particularly in view of the fact that Olana is a popular place, with some 25,000 visitors to the house annually. Admission is charged. Call (518) 828–0135 or go to www.olana.org.

Of similar interest: Other outings relating to the Hudson River painters are described in chapter 1 (West Point) and chapter 5 (Kaaterskill Falls).

Aspet: Home and Studio of Augustus Saint-Gaudens

Cornish, New Hampshire

Directions: From Boston take the Massachusetts Turnpike west to Interstate 91 north to exit 8; take Route 131 east and turn left onto Route 12A north. Aspet is located just off Route 12A in Cornish, New Hampshire; it is 12 miles north of Claremont, New Hampshire, and 2.5 miles north of the covered bridge at Windsor, Vermont.

If your idea of the nineteenth-century artist living in the depths of a city in a dreadful Bohemian garret needs changing, visit the home and studio of Augustus Saint-Gaudens. Now a National Historic Site complete with park rangers and one of the most beautiful landscapes imaginable, Aspet, the artist's summer place and eventual year-round home, is a rarely visited treasure. You may come away thinking that life as one of America's most famous sculptors must have been heavenly.

The National Park Service has made this memorial to Saint-Gaudens an elegant, tasteful, and fascinating place to visit. Though Saint-Gaudens's own experiences there were not so universally glamorous and moneyed as they now appear (the docent told us that several disastrous studio fires and a $30,000 loan to keep the place going were among the less glorious facts of Aspet's past), this estate shows off his art and architecture in a noble fashion. From the distant vistas of fields and mountains, to the charmingly columned and arbored studios, to the delicately set sculptures along garden paths, this is how we would like to imagine an illustrious artist's estate.

The site of Aspet is in rural Cornish, New Hampshire, just beyond the longest covered bridge in the nation. It crosses the Connecticut River from Vermont at Windsor. Nearby, a perfectly kept roadway into the deep woods takes you to Aspet. Despite its original use as a posting house along a traveled route, the house and its surroundings seemed to us wonderfully remote, like some Shangri-la amid the picturesque New England countryside. The large property includes a number of studios in addition to the sculptor's home, formal gardens, a deep wooded ravine, and enough fields and lawns to satisfy even a walker without a taste for sculpture. A striking view of nearby Mount Ascutney adds to the vista. But the art is, of course, the featured attraction, magnificently displayed with architecture and nature as its allies.

Augustus Saint-Gaudens was one of America's premier artists and probably its most beloved nineteenth-century sculptor. Born in 1848 in Dublin to a French shoemaker's family from the small village of Aspet in the Pyrenees, Augustus was brought to the United States as a baby. At thirteen he was apprenticed to a cameo cutter (and, in fact, his large bronze cameos later became a staple of his work; many are displayed at the estate). At nineteen he left for Europe to study art, working as a cameo cutter in Paris and Rome to support himself. In Paris he experimented with naturalistic representation and the modeling of surfaces; in Rome he studied the works of Donatello and delicate low relief.

At twenty-seven he returned home and began his American career. He worked briefly with John La Farge (as a mural painter) and began his lifelong friendships with the architects Stanford White and Charles McKim. They eventually collaborated on many projects, some of which can be seen at Aspet.

It was the commission in 1876 to create a statue commemorating Admiral David Farragut that brought Saint-Gaudens lasting recognition and success. The statue was exhibited in Paris, cast in bronze, and placed in Madison Square in New York City. Set upon Stanford White's unusual pedestal, Saint-Gaudens's unconventional, powerful figure of the admiral made him a celebrity. (A cast of this work is prominently displayed at Aspet.)

Saint-Gaudens's naturalistic approach contrasted with the smooth, controlled surfaces and contours of neoclassical sculpture that had been in vogue. By 1880 he had become an acknowledged leader of American sculptors in an era in which the memorial statue was a necessity in every city square. Other artists joined him in rejecting academicism; in 1878 he was a founder of the Society of American Artists, which sought to free both painting and sculpture from the academic and banal styles of portraiture.

His commemorative statues of famous people (including Abraham Lincoln) were in great demand and are familiar images to us today. But perhaps his best-known and most beloved work—beautifully displayed at Aspet—was his venture into a more emotional style: his *Adams Memorial.* This grieving, hooded figure is arguably the most original and haunting sculpture yet achieved by an American.

Saint-Gaudens became a widely respected teacher and leader of other artists. In 1885, after he bought the old staging inn that was to become Aspet, Cornish became the center of an artists' colony that grew up about him. (Legend has it that a friend persuaded him to go to New England in the summertime; he was then at work on an important Lincoln portrait and was told that he would find among the natives of New Hampshire many "Lincoln-shaped" men to use for models.)

Aspet became a center for both sculptors and other creative people; Saint-Gaudens's salon attracted poets, novelists, journalists, and actors. You'll find a flyer describing the Cornish Colony's illustrious members at Aspet. The artists included sculptors Frederick MacMonnies, Philip Martiny, and James Earle Fraser; among the painters were George de Forest Brush, Thomas Deming, and Maxfield Parrish.

For some twenty-two years Saint-Gaudens worked at Aspet, adding continually to the estate by building new studios and gardens and redesigning the old. During these full years he created some of his most famous works, advised presidents and museums, and won numerous international prizes and awards. (Agreeably, the displays at Aspet are devoted to his art rather than to his illustrious life as an important artist.)

Aspet became a National Historic Site in 1965, the first home of an artist to be so designated. (The second is Weir Farm; see chapter 29.) Like other national park sites, this one provides guided tours of the house and grounds, but you can also wander on your own throughout the estate (you cannot enter the house unaccompanied, however).

Begin your visit at the sculptor's home. Here, in a perfect white New England house with a grand columned veranda shaded by grape leaves, you can sit and contemplate the vista (or wait for a house tour). The house, which dates to around 1800, is small roomed and Victorian within, hardly reflecting the grandeur of Saint-Gaudens's sculptural conceptions. Deep peach- and rose-colored drapes and shades, a large faded tapestry, and dark Victorian furniture set the tone. A few small, curious paintings enliven the interior—one is by his friend and colleague Stanford White, another by the sculptor's wife.

The spectacular veranda was added to the house and is its most inviting feature. Its classical columns and magnificent view conjure visions of the Cornish Colony seated in the prevailing westerly breeze and discussing art and literature a century ago. But to begin your tour, leave the veranda from the far steps and make your way to the gardens below. Saint-Gaudens had a taste for landscape design, white marble paths, and formal gardens. Of particular note are the carefully maintained, rare clumps of mature white birches and the individually designed rectangular flower gardens.

Each part of the estate has its own plan, with borders and hedges of pine or hemlock. Small sculptured heads appear above the boxwoods here and there. There are pools, fountains that shoot jets of water through the mouths of fish and turtles (designed by the sculptor), and marble benches for the proper contemplation of it all. (The white bench decorated with figures of Pan playing his pipes is, however, the work of Augustus's brother Louis, also a sculptor of note.)

Your next stop is the Little Studio, an enchanting building that was once a hay barn. Transformed for Saint-Gaudens into a romantic workplace, the Little Studio reminds us of the sculptor's fascination with the images of antiquity. George Babb, an associate of Stanford White, redesigned the old barn into a classical Italianate structure. It has brilliant white columns now ornamented with clinging vines, contrasting with a rose-red wall (described as "Pompeiian red") and a frieze that copies the figures of the Parthenon.

Inside the Little Studio is a charming room filled with natural light. It contains small Saint-Gaudens works, including low-relief portraits, and many books; in a corner a twenty-eight-minute video of the sculptor's life is shown. (This seems to be the only modern touch, except for lawn mowers droning on the vast grounds.) Another room houses a discreet shop with memorabilia and books on the sculptor. The Little Studio is as pretty a place to picture an artist creating as you can imagine, but today there is hardly any sign that he actually worked there. (How to present a "working" studio to the public is an ongoing debate in preservationist circles.) The Little Studio also presents a series of chamber music concerts.

On leaving this building, follow the path to the *Adams Memorial* in its own garden, grandly surrounded by a square hedge and plantings. Arguably Saint-Gaudens's most stunning work, this is a cast of the original in Washington D.C. The shrouded, seated figure was commissioned by Henry Adams on the death of his wife in 1885. It is not a portrait but a symbol of mourning, and it brought American sculpture to a new depth of emotion, anticipating expressionism by many years. When the British novelist John Galsworthy saw it, he remarked that it gave him more pleasure than anything else he had seen in America, commenting, "That great greenish bronze figure of [a] seated woman within the hooding folds of her ample cloak seemed to carry [one] down to the bottom of [one's] soul."

Through the hedgerow and along the birch-lined pathway you'll see the bowling green, where family and friends lawn bowled. Next you'll come to a well-known bust of Abraham Lincoln and then to the *Shaw Memorial,* a large bronze bas-relief that commemorates the Civil War's African-American Fifty-fourth Regiment from Massachusetts. (This is a cast of the original, which stands in Boston Common.) Saint-Gaudens worked for fourteen years on this major sculpture. It is surrounded by a white grape arbor in a sun-dappled garden. Nearby is a carriage barn filled with highly polished carriages and sleighs. (Saint-Gaudens enjoyed tobogganing and other sports at Aspet.)

Returning to the path, bear left across the open lawn to the gallery. This comparatively modern building houses pretty gardens and Saint-Gaudens sculptures, as well as changing exhibitions of contemporary painting, sculpture, and photography. There is a reflecting pool in the atrium of the gallery. The sculptor originally had built a studio for his plaster molder and areas for his assistants on this site; it burned down in 1904, with the loss of many works in progress, sketchbooks, and correspondence. Its replacement was also destroyed by fire in 1944.

Among the high points of Saint-Gaudens's works in the gallery are his famous massive statue called *The Puritan* and a particularly appealing wall-size bas-relief of the ailing Robert Louis Stevenson, bedridden but nonetheless a romantic figure. The gallery for today's artists is a nice, bright space; it was showing the work of Louis Iselin during our last visit. (Needless to say, his sculptures looked shockingly modern in this nineteenth-century environment.) Outside the gallery is the *Farragut Base*, the original stone pedestal for the monumental and influential statue that brought Saint-Gaudens such celebrity. Designed in collaboration with Stanford White, it is indeed impressive with its rough texture and free form.

From here, follow the signs to the Ravine Studio, which Saint-Gaudens used occasionally. This is still a real studio where a contemporary sculptor is generally at work and will welcome you as part of the historic site's interpretative program; the artist is in residence in season weekdays from 9:00 A.M. to 4:30 P.M. It is a nice touch to see sculpture in process after so much finished work.

The estate also includes a dramatic and rather steep descent into a forested ravine. (A nature trail guide is available where you park.) If you choose to take this walk, you will find it exceptionally beautiful but be sure to wear proper shoes for a climb!

The path eventually will bring you to the bottom of the great field in front of the house, where the Cornish Colony had a Greek-style columned temple erected in 1905 to celebrate twenty years of Saint-Gaudens's residence at Aspet. It later became the family burial place.

This is but a thumbnail sketch of the many pleasures to be found at Aspet. A true student of sculpture might spend a long day noting the many works of art—some almost hidden among the shrubbery—while a nature buff could hike the paths of Aspet for an equally long time. You can choose your own pace here, perhaps resting on a marble bench in front of a well-known statue or examining the many small bas-reliefs on Saint-Gaudens's studio walls. Whatever your style, this is an artwalk to savor.

Information: The Saint-Gaudens National Historic Site is open daily from the last weekend in May through October 31. The buildings are open from 8:30 A.M. to 4:30 P.M. and the grounds from 8:00 A.M. until dark. There is an inexpensive admission fee for those over the age of sixteen. The mailing address is RR 3, Box 73, Cornish, NH 03745; telephone (603) 675–2175; Web site www.sgnhs.org.

In the vicinity: Visit the campus of Dartmouth College in Hanover, New Hampshire, to see the great Mexican painter José Clemente Orozco's murals (see chapter 42).

Windsor (almost directly across the Connecticut

River from Cornish) is known as the birthplace of Vermont; in addition to its wonderful covered bridge, it has several attractions worth noting. Windsor's historic district is composed of forty-five buildings, including several houses and a church designed by Asher Benjamin, a colonial portrait painter. The Vermont State Craft Center is in the center of town. The American Precision Museum in an old water-powered factory is intriguing; its fascinating glimpse of tools and machinery may remind you of some contemporary kinetic constructions now regarded as art. It is open May 20 to November 1, weekdays from 9:00 A.M. to 5:00 P.M. and weekends and holidays from 10:00 A.M. to 4:00 P.M.

At Bellows Falls, Vermont, you'll find another artistic curiosity: About 50 feet downriver from the Vilas Bridge, on the west side of the Connecticut River (but best viewed from the opposite side), are some interesting Indian petroglyphs. These stone pictures are incised and/or painted in yellow onto boulders at the edge of the river (you can find them just beyond the white fence). There are six heads, including a horned shaman's head thought to be the work of the Pennacook Indians.

Of similar interest: To visit the summer home and studio of Saint-Gaudens's colleague Daniel Chester French, see chapter 26.

Weir Farm: Home and Studio of J. Alden Weir

Ridgefield, Connecticut

Directions: From New York City take the Merritt Parkway to U.S. Highway 7 north, through Wilton and Branchville. Go left on Route 102, then take the second road on your left, Old Branchville Road; turn left onto Nod Hill Road to Weir Farm. The Weir Preserve is entered at either Pelham Lane or Nod Hill Road; signs are posted.

Western Connecticut is an area of gentle hills, stone walls, fine old oak trees, and red barns. Its rolling landscape is tranquil and picturesque rather than dramatic. It is the kind of place that is inviting for walkers, particularly at its greenest, in late spring or summer, when the light and the colors seem wonderfully fresh.

Not long after dozens of painters had begun flocking to Giverny in France to learn about impressionism from the master, Claude Monet, a small but significant group of Americans started painting outdoors in Connecticut, taking the first steps toward American impressionism. (In fact, Weir bought the farm six months after Monet moved to Giverny.)

These outdoor artists were brought to the area by the artist J. Alden Weir, who purchased an old farm in Branchville (now part of Ridgefield) for $10 and a still-life painting in 1882. With his colleague John Twachtman and many friends, including John Singer Sargent, Childe Hassam, and Albert Pinkham Ryder, Weir explored the Connecticut landscape. Weir and Twachtman began painting outdoors and examining light's effect on color—taking the first gentle steps toward the European style of impressionism.

Weir Farm, just recently dedicated as a National Historic Site, the first national park in Connecticut, was the scene of great artistic activity from the 1880s until Weir's death in 1919. Its studios and the surrounding landscape (a delightful stroll covering sixty-two acres) were saved from development at the last minute. Though the farm has shrunk from its original 238 acres, it is still large enough to include many a picturesque landscape, and even a lily pond that Weir built, perhaps with Giverny in mind. In order to appreciate the setting fully, however, a little bit of art history might be welcome, for Weir Farm was—in its simple, picturesque way—an important location in the development of American painting.

J. Alden Weir, the son of a drawing professor at West Point, Robert Weir (who taught both Generals Grant and Lee, by the way), and younger brother of landscapist John Ferguson Weir, was for many years a conservative, academic painter. When he went off as a young man to study art in Paris, he wrote back in 1877: "I went across the river the other day to see an exhibition of the work of a new school which call themselves 'Impressionists.' I never in my life saw more horrible things. They do not observe drawing nor form but give you an impression of what they call nature." For Weir had come from an American academic artistic background, painting realistic topographical scenes and giving drawing and form major importance in his compositions. The hazy impressionistic painting that he saw abroad opposed the principles he brought with him from America. He shared America's anti-European feeling about "foreign" styles of art, though he—like all young artists—went there for traditional art study.

On his return to the United States, Weir settled in New York, where he was a successful painter of delicate, naturalistic still lifes, flower pieces, portraits, and domestic scenes. But he was a great nature lover, having been raised on Emerson and "back to nature" themes. In 1883 he moved his family to the farm in Connecticut to escape urban life; soon the beauty of his surroundings beckoned him to begin outdoor painting. Before long, Weir—a gregarious and magnetic figure in the art world—had brought other painters to his home in Branchville. He was to paint there every summer for thirty-seven years. By 1890 he and Twachtman were experimenting with impressionistic canvases of scenes on the farm, using pure colors from the prism to create the sense of flickering light and impressionistic changes in the atmosphere. They became so excited by outdoor painting that they even devised a portable winter studio. (You will see the sites of these forays on the farm when you visit.)

Weir went on to organize and guide the Ten, a loosely knit but nonetheless influential group of American impressionists. Their collective withdrawal from the established exhibitions in New York City to show their works together was a revolutionary moment in American painting. But Weir and his colleagues did not consider themselves rebels. They never abandoned entirely their American artistic roots; American impressionism retained its interest in the factual (though Weir never minded adding or transposing a tree or flower—he called it "hollyhocking"). Their paintings and explorations of light were an outgrowth of the tradition of luminism in American art, and they saw their experiments in painting light through the use of prismatic color as a natural step forward. They never issued a manifesto of impressionism, nor sought to make dramatic political statements. Both Weir and Twachtman, as well as their colleagues in the Ten, were somewhat surprised by their designation as American impressionists.

Weir Farm became a center for artists, and Weir himself held open-air classes. Nearby Cos Cob soon became an art colony, where his friends took summer homes. Weir was a busy man, painting, teaching, encouraging and supporting his colleagues, and serving on the board of the Metropolitan Museum of Art and as president of the National Academy of Design. His personal charm and dynamism (he was known as "the diplomat") enabled him to move the static world of academic art forward, without dramatic means or revolutionary art.

Weir lived at the farm until his death. His daughter married the sculptor Mahonri Young, who built the beautiful second studio and continued to work there. Your tour of the farm will include studios used by both artists and a variety of memorabilia from both of their careers.

Since Weir Farm was only recently dedicated as a National Historic Site, its full program is not completely in place. (The house is still occupied by an artist, who will show it on designated days.) The grounds are always open for walking, however. We particularly liked the studios, with their clutter and confusion, including friezes, potbellied stoves, plaster casts, old photos, souvenirs, shelves of still life, and quite a bit of nice carved wainscoting. An addition houses etching machinery and armatures and bookbinding materials. We recommend visiting on a day when the studios are open so that you can see them all.

Plans for the future of Weir Farm include rotating exhibitions, artists working on-site, and lectures and classes. We hope that the powers-that-be will leave the studios as they are, rather than clean them up to resemble some fictitious studios where an artist might never have dropped a spot of paint on the floor. In fact, the tranquillity of Weir Farm can only be retained with the most careful management. This is not yet a tourist attraction, and—for the sake of both art lovers and walkers—we hope it stays the way it is.

In order to visit Weir Farm's buildings, you must telephone for an appointment with a guide. (When we visited, the guide was the artist-in-residence.) When you arrive, you will receive a map and walking guide that identifies the sites and views of some of Weir's Branchville paintings, and you can wander off to find them on your own. His 1905 painting *Upland Pasture* (National Museum of American Art, Smithsonian Institution) pictures an area that is still part of the property and looks remarkably the same. Other views of the farm painted by Weir and his colleagues include the barns, the pond, laundry on a line, and trees in the snow.

You will also find a nature preserve adjacent to Weir Farm. The Weir Preserve consists of 110 additional acres of unspoiled Connecticut landscape given by the artist's daughter and several other residents of the area. A map with listings of wildflowers and trees is available at Weir Farm.

Information: Weir Farm is located in southwestern Connecticut in the towns of Ridgefield and Wilton. The grounds are open year-round Monday through Friday from 8:30 A.M. to 5:00 P.M. The studios are open one day a month (usually on a Thursday) during spring, summer, and fall. Admission is charged. For information call (203) 834–1896 or visit www.nps.gov/wefa.

In the vicinity: For a complete change of pace, visit the nearby Aldrich Museum of Contemporary Art at 258 Main Street in Ridgefield. This attractive museum is particularly noted for its modern sculpture garden and for its very trendy changing exhibitions. Without visiting the galleries in New York City, you can get a taste of the latest in avant-garde paintings, sculptures, and constructions. Of special interest is its outdoor sculpture collection. Using a map (available at the desk), you can spot large works by Tony Rosenthal, Arnaldo Pomodoro, Robert Morris, Lila Katzen, David Von Schlegel, Sol LeWitt, Alexander Liberman, and other contemporary sculptors and construction artists. There is an entrance fee for the museum, but the sculpture garden can be seen separately without going indoors. Call (203) 438–4519 for information.

Of similar interest: For more American impressionist art sites in Connecticut, see chapter 25 (Old Lyme and Cos Cob).

Locust Grove: Home, Studio, and Grounds of Samuel F. B. Morse

Poughkeepsie, New York

Directions: From New York City take the Henry Hudson Parkway north to the Saw Mill River Parkway to the Taconic State Parkway. Take the exit for Poughkeepsie (Route 55) and go west for several miles, almost to the Mid Hudson Bridge, then take U.S. Highway 9 south for about 2 miles. The entrance to Locust Grove is on your right.

For an outing focusing on the extraordinary career of a true nineteenth-century phenomenon, Samuel F. B. Morse, we take you to Locust Grove. Located on a bluff above the Hudson, just south of Poughkeepsie, this National Historic Site is a pleasure and provides a fascinating glimpse into the life of both an artist and inventor.

A visit to Locust Grove is unique because it combines Morse's interests in new technology with his consummate skill as a painter. The Morse code and the machine for telegraphing it, known as the "invention of the century," caused him to be called the "American Leonardo." You can see a replica of this machine at the visitor center. Here you'll also find sculptures and numerous paintings—mostly portraits but also landscapes—as well as collections relating to his life at Locust Grove. In the wonderful redesigned Italianate mansion (inspired by Morse's 1829 painting tour of Italy), which became his summer home in 1847, are collections of Chippendale, Federal, and Empire–style furnishings, as well as artworks by other painters: Dutch landscapes, Hudson River School paintings, and even twentieth-century works.

Surrounding this beautifully set house are 150 acres of trees, spacious lawns, and gardens, with 3 miles of walking trails and a looping carriage roadway. The grounds are scenically dramatic, with river views from the bluff (in Morse's time there were fewer trees to block the view of the majestic Hudson). Pick up a self-guided tour brochure, which will introduce you to the sites to visit, including the dog cemetery! You can see the house by taking a forty-five-minute (approximately) guided tour.

Morse was the founder of the National Academy of Design (in 1825) and taught "literature of the art of design" at New York University. His finely drawn paintings established him as a preeminent artist of the American Romantic school, but when he became famous for his invention, he abandoned painting and was able to enjoy a life of ease, as this villa and its grounds testify. Morse is known as an important painter of his era and as a major inventor; a visit here will introduce you to both aspects of this unusual dual career.

Information: Locust Grove is located at 2683 South Road (US 9), Poughkeepsie. The gardens and grounds are open dawn to dusk year-round; house tours are offered daily May through November from 10:00 A.M. to 3:00 P.M. Admission is charged. Call (845) 454–4500 or go to www.morsehistoricsite.org.

In the vicinity: Beacon, a few miles south on US 9, is home to DIA Beacon, one of the newest and most spectacular contemporary art sites in our area. The museum, a converted factory with some 300,000 square feet of exhibition space, features art from the 1960s to the present, with an emphasis on pop and conceptual art by well-known American artists. Open year-round; call for hours (845–440–0100).

Of similar interest: Other artists' homes and studios open to the public in the region include the Thomas Cole House and Olana (see chapter 27) and the houses/studios of Jasper Cropsey and Russel Wright (see chapter 24).

31

East Hampton's Artistic Heritage and the Pollock-Krasner House and Study Center

East Hampton, New York

Directions: From New York City take the Long Island Expressway, then Route 111 to Route 27 east to East Hampton.

The fabled Hamptons of the Long Island coast conjure up ocean vistas, wide unspoiled beaches, soft sea breezes, and broad encompassing skies. This elegant string of colonial shore villages, once surrounded by vast potato fields (few of which remain), has long delighted visitors. Celebrities, whose dramatic beachside homes and legendary parties are routinely chronicled in gossip columns and glossy magazines, summer here. Day-trippers come for the pleasures of sea, sun, and people watching, while others are simply here to enjoy a spot of great natural beauty in what can also be a quiet, peaceful environment.

But the Hamptons are more than a glorious playground for weekend and summer pleasure seekers. Artists have long been seduced by the timeless views that can still be enjoyed at every turn. They have lived and worked here—in East Hampton, Southampton, Bridgehampton, and their environs—since the mid-nineteenth century. The list is long and impressive. Thomas Moran, the great American landscapist, was one of the first to paint here. Childe Hassam followed at the turn of the twentieth century, as did William Merritt Chase; the painter Lucia Cox, a protégé of F. Scott Fitzgerald's friends Gerald and Sara Murphy, brought Fernand Léger and Max Ernst; and Peggy Guggenheim and a coterie of surrealists arrived during World War II.

The notable husband-and-wife abstract expressionist painters Jackson Pollock and Lee Krasner moved to the Springs, near East Hampton, in the mid-1940s. They were soon joined in the area by other abstract expressionists, including such seminal figures as Elaine and Willem de Kooning, Robert Motherwell, David Hare, and Harold and May Rosenberg, and the newly revitalized Hamptons became one of the country's premier art colonies. Today little remains to be seen of the expressionists' heyday, with the exception of the Pollock-Krasner House and Study Center, now a cultural center filled with art and memorabilia and open to the public.

Although the heady era of the abstract expressionists is long past, the area has continued to attract artists and patrons. The Jimmy Ernst Artist's Alliance lists as many as 500 artists working in every imaginable style, and the Guild Hall in East Hampton has large annual shows. Fortunately for the visitor to the area, a number of painters and sculptors open their studios by appointment. You might also want to make time to explore on foot the delightful village of East Hampton, which has retained much of its colonial character. Its often-photographed windmills, stately old homes, and town pond add to its picturesque charms.

The best time to plan your visit is in early summer or after Labor Day. Midsummer is the time the Hamptons are abuzz with frenetic activity; the traffic within the towns can be daunting and parking more of a challenge than you might wish (particularly in East Hampton). One pleasant way to avoid this aggravation is to park your car away from the main congestion, unload your bike (or rent one in town), and pedal your way from one art site to the next. You'll find the scenery, setting, and flat roads perfectly suited to bicycling.

The Guild Hall, the town's cultural center, right on Main Street, is definitely worth a stop. Here the works of Long Island artists, past and present, are on display. Since some of these artists are well-known, shows here invariably have more than regional appeal. Changing summer exhibits, including a summer sculpture show in the garden, feature the work of living area artists. (Such noted figures as Audrey Flack, James Brooks, and Larry Rivers live in the area.) The permanent collection, shown from October 1 to May 31, displays not only work by contemporary local artists, but also that of older masters who painted here, such as Thomas Moran, Childe Hassam, and Jackson Pollock.

From here head east on Main Street, bearing left just below the windmill onto North Main Street. Take the right-hand fork marked SPRINGS FIREPLACE to Springs Fireplace Road. A mile or so down the road will take you to our major site, the Pollock-Krasner House and Study Center at 830 Fireplace Road. In 1945 Pollock and Krasner moved to this small, unpretentious nineteenth-century white clapboard farmhouse in the fishing community known as "The Springs." It was here, in this idyllic setting overlooking Accabonac Creek and Gardiners Bay, that Pollock created the famous masterworks that so changed the direction of contemporary art.

In 1987 the center was established as a museum and research

facility. The museum includes the main house as well as Pollock's studio, beautifully situated in a charming garden. The studio, a converted barn, displays a collection of vintage photos that document the lives and working methods of both Pollock and Krasner. Their working materials have been kept intact, just as they were when last used, in a somewhat shrinelike manner. You can even walk across Pollock's famous paint-splattered floor.

In the main house the couple's living quarters are kept as they were in the 1950s, filled with Victorian furniture and a vast collection of jazz recordings and books. The huge art reference library is devoted primarily to the birth of abstract expressionism, with a particular emphasis on those artists who lived and worked in this part of eastern Long Island. There is also an oral history collection and videos relating the heyday of abstract expressionism. Students and scholars use this facility, but it is also open to the public. Tours are offered, as well as many classes and events; call for information before you go.

Information: The Guild Hall, on Main Street in East Hampton, is open year-round; call (631) 324–0806. The Pollack-Krasner House and Study Center is at 830 Fireplace Road in East Hampton. It is open May, September, and October by appointment only, with guided tours given Thursday, Friday, and Saturday on the hour from 11:00 A.M. to 4:00 P.M. In June, July, and August, it is open by appointment on Thursday, Friday, and Saturday at 11:00 A.M. for a guided tour; general admission (no appointment required) is from 1:00 to 5:00 P.M. Admission is charged. Call (631) 324–4929 or go to http://naples.cc.sunysb.edu/CAS/pkhouse.nsf.

In the vicinity: Visit the Parrish Art Museum at 25 Jobs Lane, Southampton, for its superb collection of nineteenth- and twentieth-century American paintings and prints, as well as Renaissance works. Don't miss the sculpture garden, which is also noted for its unusual tree specimens. Admission is free. Call (516) 283–2118 or visit www.parrishart.org for hours (they vary seasonally) and additional information.

Outdoor Collections:
Art in Public Settings

32

Pyramids, Gothic Arches, and Classical Temples at West Laurel Hill Cemetery

Bala-Cynwyd, Pennsylvania

Directions: From Philadelphia take Interstate 76 west from the Walt Whitman Bridge. About 7 miles from the bridge, take exit 31 (City Avenue); continue on City Avenue to Belmont Avenue and turn right. After the second intersection, look for the entrance gate on the right.

It may surprise you to find a cemetery as a site for an art or architecture walk, but this is not an ordinary cemetery. A walk through West Laurel Hill, in Bala-Cynwyd, near South Philadelphia, is like a fantastic tour through the history of architecture. Not only is the natural scenery spectacular—there are more than 150 species of trees, many of which blossom in season—but there are mausoleums in styles ranging from Egyptian pyramids to Greek temples to miniature Gothic chapels.

A walk around this very large area is filled with intriguing sights, beautiful views, and food for thought: Who were these people who were buried like kings in nineteenth-century America? Where did they get such curious ideas of art and architecture—combining Egyptian or classical Greek tomb styles with the brilliant colors of art nouveau stained glass or the whimsical design of Moorish ironwork? (Postmodernism seems to have been preinvented at West Laurel Hill!) Why does the ornamentation include so many references to ancient Egyptian and classical mythology in these nominally Christian tombs?

Many of the mausoleums are dramatic, imposing, and grand, yet they are still miniatures; two of them are replicas of the Parthenon. As you walk through the graceful landscape, you feel almost as though you are Gulliver in a small mythical city. In fact, the sense of being in another time and place is pervasive; there are few visitors (we were there on weekdays), nothing to read (there are almost no inscriptions beyond the names of the honored dead), and the stillness is broken only by the sound of the wind in the giant old trees. You can walk up to the "entrances" of many of the tombs (which, of course, are never entered) and peer into their empty interiors to see the colorful stained-glass light, or sit on one of the numerous walls or stone stairways to draw or contemplate your surroundings without interruption.

West Laurel Hill Cemetery was originally a country estate on the outskirts of Philadelphia, about 4 miles from the city. In 1869 the hilly spot was purchased by some leading citizens for use as a cemetery; it was to provide a safely removed and inspirational spot for contemplation of nature and God. (Cemeteries like West Laurel Hill became models—with their design of pathways, plantings, and open space—for the great public parks that appeared in the nation's cities in the nineteenth century.) Because of the cemetery's situation beyond the city limits, transportation there was difficult in the early days. Funerals took all day, with excursions by steamboat on the Schuylkill River or by carriage up to the high bluffs of the cemetery. Eventually railway cars were employed to carry funeral corteges. As you will see from the names on the tombs, leading citizens of Philadelphia's business and social world chose this cemetery as their last resting place. By the turn of the twentieth century, it had become a testament not only to worldly success but to the Victorian fascination with grandeur—both in art and nature.

A walk through the grounds poses some problems. The area is very large, and you will necessarily have to leave out some of the walkways unless you have a great deal of time. The old carriage roads cover more than one hundred acres of hill and dale. It is possible to drive through most of the cemetery if you wish, but you will be unable to leave your car along the way, so we recommend parking at the office lot in the center of the grounds. You can then follow our route to see the tombs we thought most interesting, or if you prefer, wander at random.

As you walk you may note—in addition to the particular sites described—some sixty-two obelisks, numerous marble statues and urns covered with ivy, several sets of classical columns unattached to buildings, and a recurrent architectural detail at the top of the facade of many temples: the Egyptian winged sun disk, or Winged Ba (representing the soul), occasionally intertwined with snakes. You will also spot Doric, Ionic, and Corinthian columns; Gothic arches and spires; and a marvelous collection of doors. These portals to the tombs are in every conceivable style, some echoing the design of the windows within, others in ironwork of Moorish or art deco design. Be sure to go up the steps to look beyond the doors at the great variety of stained glass inside many of the mausoleums. While most tombs are built of marble, you will also find sandstone and granite;

the overall impression is of sparkling white buildings set against an extraordinarily green landscape.

One additional note before you begin: Don't overlook the trees and shrubbery. The natural beauty of the 187 acres is astounding. Many of the trees were planted more than a hundred years ago. Among the 150 species are a 65-foot-tall magnolia shadowing a grave marked CARPENTER, flowering dogwood, cherry, weeping beech, sweetgum, oak, birch, euonymous, sugar maple, fern maple, and copper beech. You'll also find flowering shrubs in season, from mauve hydrangea, azalea, and rhododendron to (of course) a profusion of laurel. Colors are particularly grand in spring and fall.

As you drive through the gate, you will see painted arrows on the roadway directing you to the office. Follow them and park in the lot in front of the beautiful ivied tower and the brick office building. At the office you can buy a history of the famous people buried in the cemetery and pick up a detailed map (which, however, includes no names or guide points).

Directly bordering the parking area are two side-by-side graves marked SOULAS and PIDGEON. We begin with these two graves because they typify the neoclassical style, an emphasis that you will see time and again on this walk. Both are distinctive for the classical mourning female figures behind glass-topped graves. (The tombs appear empty when you look into their 15-foot depth.)

Turn to your left to find the first large mausoleum on our walk. It is a monument to Frederick August Poth, a very successful German-born brewer. This classical revival structure is marble with symmetrical Corinthian columns, flanges, and urns. It is massive and impressive and dates to 1905.

If you continue on the pathway to the left of the Poth tomb, you will come to a row of some of the cemetery's most interesting mausoleums. Here you'll find the Greek Revival style in a number of forms, most including stained glass in an art nouveau mode. Be sure to go up the steps of each and peek in to see the widely divergent styles of the glass and the doorways.

In addition to the Greek Revival designs along this row, there are also two interesting mausoleums showing Moorish influence. One of them is the John Lang monument, a curious blend of Moorish and classical design; note the carved decoration. Across from it (and slightly farther along) is the Coane monument. This one, which contrasts with its neoclassical neighbors, looks rather like a beehive.

Just behind the Coane monument is a grave marked STETSON. Though it is not of particular architectural interest, you may like to know where the founder of Stetson hats is buried! Also on the right side of this roadway—but somewhat behind this row—is the very distinctive tomb of Matthew Simpson (1811–1884), a bishop of the Methodist Episcopal Church. His mausoleum is a replica of a Gothic chapel, complete with a Gothic arch, trefoil (intersecting circles symbolizing the Trinity), and Latin cross. Note the fine stained-glass windows, which include a New Testament scene, a fleur-de-lis, and a Star of David.

If you return to the same pathway, opposite and somewhat farther along, you'll find the Eisenlohr monument, one of the cemetery's finest Greek Revival examples. It is not only distinguished in its architectural detail, but also has unusually nice stained glass in the art nouveau style within.

At the end of this section of roadway is a monument marked HARRAH. Charles J. Harrah (1817–1890) was a steel and railway magnate and humanitarian who personified the successful nineteenth-century industrialist. His career took him to Brazil, where he developed railways and shipyards as well as that country's first public school. His mausoleum is appropriately grand, with its Victorian Gothic spires and ornamentation. Its design is based upon a series of rounded and pointed arches culminating in a spire with a cross at the top. It has been likened to the Prince Albert Memorial in London and is what used to be known as an "architectural confection."

Returning to the intersecting paths at the Harrah memorial, take the narrow path and climb up the hill. At the top, to your right, you'll come upon several interesting mausoleums overlooking lower areas of the cemetery. First you'll see the Alter monument, whose unusual stained-glass windows pick up the intricate Moorish design of the wrought-iron door.

Surrounding this tomb are two oddities: large white marble chairs that look like bizarre monuments themselves. They were placed on private lots by some long-forgotten grave site owners to provide a view of the hillside and, presumably, a place for meditation and prayer. In their peculiar juxtaposition with the varied tombs and monuments, however, they seem like works of art placed by some twentieth-century sculptor in an unlikely place. There are several other such monuments at West Laurel Hill.

On the same path is a distinctive and very ornate art nouveau tomb dedicated to John P. Mathieu. Note the St. John the Baptist windows, the curlicues on the roof, the stylish arched door, and the matching decorative flowerpots.

Go back to the intersection and continue in the same direction until you come to the Berwind memorial. Another well-known capitalist, Edward J. Berwind was a naval aide to President Grant and became one of the largest individual owners of coal mines in the country. Berwind's mausoleum is notable: It was designed by the famous architect Horace Trumbauer (who is also buried at West

Laurel Hill). It is a striking, tall, octagonal tower, with neoclassical winged figures in a bas-relief circling the eight sides.

In a nearby parallel row is one of two monuments to the Pew family. The mausoleum of Joseph Newton Pew, the founder of the Sun Company, resembles a neoclassical temple, with graceful proportions and elegant surfaces. Just around the bend is another Pew monument; though there is no temple, this one is nevertheless another evocation of ancient Greece. It consists of linked marble columns set in a lovely site, surrounded with greenery.

Following the map, climb to one of the highest and most beautiful spots at West Laurel Hill. Here the founder of the Campbell Soup Company, John T. Dorrance, is honored with a flat-roofed neoclassical temple. Its imposing entranceway between Ionic columns was placed on the long side of its oblong shape, giving it a massive facade. Dorrance, one of the world's richest people during his lifetime (1919–1989), was a patron of the Philadelphia Museum of Art and an art collector himself. Next to the Dorrance mausoleum on the hilltop is another tomb belonging to the same family.

Continue along this roadway to get a quick glimpse of one of the largest (but not particularly interesting architecturally) tombs on the tour. This huge building honors a public-utility magnate named Clarence H. Geist. His mausoleum is a massive, somber white cube.

Beyond the Geist memorial, on a pathway to your left, is a row with three tombs of interest. The first (on your right) is an Ionic-style temple that is a miniature replica of the Parthenon, though it is hardly miniature; this grand mausoleum is dedicated to Edward M. Story. A bit farther along, on your left, is the J. Howell Cummings mausoleum, a particularly nice example of stylish 1920s architecture, with its soft peach and gray facade and elegant doors decorated with sheaves of wheat.

Next you'll come to a curiosity: Algernon Sidney Logan's obelisk and temple. Logan (1849–1925) was a poet and novelist, and the titles of his books are incised on the marble obelisk, along with a clock face whose hands are set at three o'clock, the time he died. This is one of many obelisks throughout the cemetery. Note the variety of styles, particularly at the topmost points.

Finally in this area you'll come upon a sandstone castle-style mausoleum with a wrought-iron gate. This is quite unlike the pale-toned tombs that fill most of the grounds. Instead, this one—dedicated to George Miller—is distinctive for its deep sand color and its somewhat medieval appearance.

From here, walk up the left path to a three-way intersection, where you'll come to one of our favorite architectural examples: the Henry M. Schadewald mausoleum (on the left). This unusual building is a Moorish design that seems to have been inspired by *Arabian Nights*. Its beautiful doorway is a series of art deco arabesques made of iron. Don't miss this one.

Opposite, just across the intersection, is one of the most intriguing of all the mausoleums at West Laurel Hill Cemetery. The Drake family (two of whose members survived the sinking of the *Titanic*) is interred here in an Egyptian-style temple set on a small knoll. This strange structure boasts a number of apparent Egyptian symbols, including the four statues at the corners of the roof, lotus flowers carved into the facade, and the winged sun disk over the entrance. In addition to the Egyptian theme, the architect added some ancient Greek symbols for good measure; the four statues that seem to be Egyptian sphinxes (male lions with human heads) are, in fact, winged lionesses, a Greek adaptation of a Near Eastern motif.

This odd mausoleum was moved from the city cemetery, bodies and all, and reconstructed at its present site.

On the same side of the roadway, on your left, is another Egyptian-influenced mausoleum, dedicated to John Kenworthy. This one also bears Egyptian symbols and ornamentation. A bit farther on the same path is one of the oddest of all the mausoleums at West Laurel Hill. This Theban-style tomb is in the shape of a flat-topped pyramid, a rather ungainly curiosity. It bears the name Charles E. Ellis, a streetcar tycoon.

Follow the curving path to a curious mausoleum just down some little stone steps from the Harrah monument. Here you'll find an eccentric tomb with the name Avery D. Harrington. This little building bears medieval symbols in an almost modernistic setting. The geometric, horizontal pattern of the door is reflected in the design of the stained-glass window within.

Continuing on this path, you will head back toward the office complex. But shortly before you reach it, stop to see the Dingee tomb, an extremely graceful neoclassical example; it is another replica of the Parthenon. From here, turn right at the next intersection, toward the giant green-domed mausoleum dominating the vista just ahead. One of the largest and most imposing mausoleums in the entire cemetery, this is the tomb of John F. Betz, a beer company magnate. It is a beautifully proportioned building in the grand nineteenth-century French style. It reminded us of the wonderful buildings on the Boulevard Haussmann in Paris—in miniature, of course—with its solemn symmetry, neoclassical columns, and lovely domed roof topped with a winged figure. Be sure to walk all the way around it.

Not far from the Betz mausoleum you'll spot two curiosities: a pair of graves marked JONES and PLATT. Both are stone markers in the shape of tree trunks, quite realistically carved, and surrounded by smaller stones. Another such tree memorial is the Kugler monument, a large granite tree trunk fronted by four granite logs. All of these markers struck us as very odd and rather modern in concept, though we understand that there is an old tradition of using tree trunk forms as memorials.

Nearby and slightly up the hill is another peculiar tomb, also reminiscent of France. This is the Cornelius Harrigan monument. It is in the French Empire style, shaped like Napoleon's tomb in the Hôtel des Invalides in Paris.

Returning to the pathway, continue toward the office (which can be seen in the distance), but take the road that goes behind it. Go down the hill to spot an interesting monument to a family of sculptors. Slightly off the path is a Celtic cross honoring the Calder family. Though the mobile maker, Alexander Calder, is not buried here, both his father, Alexander Sterling Calder, and his grandfather, Alexander Milne Calder, are. They were well-known artists whose works grace both Philadelphia's and New York's public spaces. The cross, which bears the names of various other Calders as well, is notable for the carving in its Scottish granite. The cross has a distinctive intertwined pattern of rosettes, as well as the traditional circle intersecting the arms of the cross. Be sure to walk fully around this monument and not to miss the Celtic writing on the front.

If you haven't had enough walking, you might like to search out the graves of a few other prominent Philadelphians: Jean August Girard (founder of Girard College), a glass-enclosed bust on a pedestal; Dave Garroway (radio and television host); Raymond Pace Alexander (noted African-American judge); Cyrus Curtis (founder of the Curtis magazine empire); Catherine Drinker Bowen (biographer and historian); Loren C. Eiseley (philosopher and anthropologist); Robert C. Grier (a Supreme Court justice during the Civil War); Herman Haupt (a Civil War general); Anna M. Jarvis (founder of Mother's Day, in 1908); Frank Maguire Mayo (famous actor of the late nineteenth century); Alfred James Reach (a founding father of baseball); Fritz Scheel (conductor and founder of the Philadelphia Orchestra); Justus Strawbridge and Isaac Clothier (of department store fame); and Horace Trumbauer (architect of many of Philadelphia's great public buildings, including the Museum of Art). If you particularly wish to find any of these grave sites, the helpful folks in the office will look them up for you and direct you to them.

Information: West Laurel Hill Cemetery is open Monday through Saturday from 8:00 A.M. to 4:00 P.M. and Sunday and holidays from 9:00 A.M. to 4:00 P.M. Call (610) 664–1591.

In the vicinity: Just northwest of Philadelphia, the township of Abingdon has transformed Alverthorpe Manor, an old and gloriously landscaped estate, into the Abingdon Art Center (515 Meetinghouse Road, Jenkintown; 215–887–4882), a magnificent space for open-air sculpture and an ongoing environmental art project. A veranda behind the charming stone manor house looks out on a vast greensward, set with modern sculptures. This is a good walk if you wish to view each artwork close up.

The featured artists are well known in the world of contemporary sculpture, but Abingdon also offers juried shows for "emerging" sculptors from the Delaware Valley area. A recent exhibition, *Out of the Blue*, featured art inspired by changing weather, but no matter what show is on view when you visit, you will find a wide variety of contemporary styles and ideas awaiting you in the luxuriously landscaped gardens.

In addition, you will want to visit the site of one of the more unusual art setups we have encountered. In a wooded area of the estate, we found a sculptor and landscape artist named Winifred Lutz working away. Deep among the fallen trees, roots, overgrown bushes, and piles of leaves, she attempted to "re-evoke a sense of woodland history by reclaiming the land." The artist restored one or two acres, making "a register of wood that has fallen" and several large installations involving the fallen tree trunks and paths that follow the footsteps of deer.

The University of Pennsylvania's Morris Arboretum (100 Northwestern Avenue, Philadelphia; 215–247–5777) is located in a greenbelt well outside the city. This is a lovely, hilly park, filled with both flowers and sculptures. Though the plantings and pathways are quintessentially Victorian in style and some of the prettiest we have seen, the sculptures are anything but old-fashioned. In fact, you might consider most of them totally unrelated to their surroundings.

The artworks are somewhat dwarfed by the magnificence of the landscape. The Butcher Sculpture Garden contains predominantly contemporary art, of which there are about a dozen permanently installed sculptures. Several Cotswold sheep made of two-dimensional Cor-Ten steel by Charles Layland are "grazing" at the base of Magnolia Slope. A kinetic steel sculpture by George Rickey called *Two Lines* moves in the wind. You'll see several constructivist pieces on the grounds, including Israel Hadany's *Three Tubes*, Buky Schwartz's *Four Cut Stones*, and an untitled painted metal sculpture by George Sugarman. Linda Cunningham is represented by *Germination*, a giant bronze and steel sculpture that evokes the garden idea.

At the center of the sculpture garden is a group of

modern works by Scott Sherk based upon classical Greek mythology (but without classical visual connotations). Robert Engman is represented with a rotating geometric sculpture called *After B.K.S. Iyengar* (a yoga master); Thomas Sternal, by two wood sculptures from felled trees, *Table* and *Altarpiece*.

The Morris collection also features several more traditional pieces, including portrait sculptures of the Morrises themselves. Children will enjoy Lorraine Vail's whimsical animal characters, including a 5-foot frog and a bull.

33

Masterworks on Campus at Princeton University

Princeton, New Jersey

Directions: Take the New Jersey Turnpike to exit 9, and take U.S. Highway 1 south, then Route 571 west to Princeton. Follow the signs for the university.

American college campuses are well known for charming shaded walks and Gothic buildings. Few, however, can compare with Princeton University's beautiful campus, nor—of particular interest for us—with its outdoor sculpture collection. Princeton has acquired an unusually fine selection of contemporary sculptures over the last decades. These works have been placed with great care among the campus's walkways and lawns, making an expedition to see them a most attractive, and artistically satisfying, artwalk.

You'll see the jagged forms of a Lipchitz against a background of buildings, a huge Picasso in front of Princeton's fine art museum, the gently moving kinetic forms by George Rickey on an open lawn, and works by David Smith, Louise Nevelson, and Isamu Noguchi, among many others. In all, some twenty-one sculptures are to be found on campus, aside from the major collection in the art museum (also open to the public).

If you enjoy strolling on a campus and looking at sculpture as you go (along with the endlessly fascinating scenes of college life around you), this tour will definitely be a favorite, to which you will return many times. We recommend a thorough visit to the art museum in conjunction with your walk, for this museum has an outstanding collection of antiquities, European and American paintings, African sculptures, and many other treasures; it is used by scholars from the university and around the world. Following, however, is specifically a sculpture walk.

Enter the university campus from Nassau Street at the gate opposite Palmer Square. You must go on foot. Park at a meter in town, or leave your car at the university parking lot and take the shuttle bus to campus. The guard at the gate will direct you to the lot or to town parking. Pick up a campus map at the information desk near the gate before you start. (Numbers in this walk refer to this map.)

A fitting beginning to this tour of twentieth-century sculpture is Henry Moore's *Oval with Points*. This commissioned work was installed in 1971 between Stanhope Hall and West College, at F2 on the map. It is made of bronze, its inside surface now burnished from contact with the thousands of students who have lounged on it (to the sculptor's delight). The sculpture bears some resemblance to an elephant skull that was given to Moore by Sir Julian Huxley and placed in the sculptor's garden. "Henry," wrote Huxley, "not only took it to his heart but proceeded to explore its massive outline, its tunnels and cavities, its recesses and blind eye-sockets . . ." You will find the Moore easily recognizable, with or without the knowledge of its relationship to the elephant skull, and you'll enjoy its graceful placement on the green.

An entirely different sculptural experience awaits you at your next stop. Walk away from the gate to the pathway behind West College, and turn left on the path. At F3 on the map you'll see the slightly undulating forms of George Rickey's *Two Planes, Vertical Horizon II*. Don't miss the Rickey work; it is just off the pathway and somewhat above your head, where its kinetic parts catch the breeze and move almost imperceptibly. You'll want to back away to look at it. Rickey is perhaps the leading exponent of this type of sculpture today, though it was Alexander Calder, whose work you will shortly see, who led the way in inventing kinetic sculpture.

Continue on the path, and turn left at its end. Between the University Chapel and Firestone Library (at G2) you'll see the Jacques Lipchitz sculpture called *Song of the Vowels*, one of a series in which the artist worked with a harp motif. This soaring bronze is a cubist structure suggesting a harpist in Lipchitz's familiar curvilinear style. The artist said that the title had to do with a legendary prayer of ancient Egypt in which the forces of nature were called upon. It was installed on the campus in 1969.

In the lobby of Firestone Library itself is another work by a master of contemporary sculpture, Isamu Noguchi. *White Sun* is one in a series of works in various media portraying the sun that the sculptor created in the 1960s. Made of white marble, it is a large irregular circle with an open center, like many Noguchi sculptures that explore circular and disc-shaped forms.

When you leave the lobby to go back outdoors, you'll see another modern "classic" between the library building and Nassau Street bordering the campus (also G2). This is *Atmosphere and Environment X* by Louise Nevelson, whose work may be recognizable to you from many of the other sculpture walks in this book. Nevelson, a major figure in contemporary sculpture, described her works in her own way: "Say an architect builds a house. Well, now let's say that he builds the whole thing inside, all the rooms and everything, but he doesn't have an outside wall. Well, it's not a house, it's a veranda. I want the total house, I don't want my sculpture to be a veranda".

Like other Nevelsons, this one is made of Cor-Ten steel and is quite large—21 feet high and 16 feet long. It is made up of interlocking black, white, and gold geometric shapes set in a shallow relief-like form. You will enjoy watching the play of light and shadow on it if you happen to have a sunny day for your walk, but it is an impressive and monumental work under any conditions. It was Nevelson's first major work in Cor-Ten steel, a medium that was to become a hallmark of her sculpture.

Between Firestone Library and Dickinson Hall (still G2), you'll discover George Segal's memorial to the Kent State massacre: *Abraham and Isaac, in Memory of May 4, 1970, Kent State University*. Segal's very realistic style is in clear contrast to the abstract sculptures we have just seen; his human figures look strikingly real, and though they represent biblical figures, their contemporary message is quite clear.

Walk along Washington Road toward the School of Architecture (G3). If you wish to go inside the building, you'll find in the stairwell Eduardo Paolozzi's imaginative *Marok, Marok, Miosa,* a contemporary work. Paolozzi was the principal exponent of England's junk sculpture movement, making works from found objects.

Here you might gauge your energy and decide whether to cross Washington Road and head several blocks across the campus to the Engineering Quadrangle, where three more sculptures are situated. If you want to make this detour, you will walk along Prospect Avenue to Olden Street, where you will turn left and continue until you reach the Engineering School (J2).

At the entrance to the quadrangle you'll see Clement Meadmore's *Upstart 2*, a work made in 1970. This minimalist form, also made of Cor-Ten steel, could be said to resemble a letter of the alphabet or a hard-edged snake; it rises from a slab base, giving an impression of surprising lightness. Meadmore is said to see his sculpture "as being like a person who inhabits a place."

While in the Engineering Quad you can see two more works (both K2): Masayuki Nagare's *Stone Riddle*, a contemporary example by the well-known Japanese artist, and *Spheric Theme* by Naum Gabo, a leading figure in Russia's early modern style of constructivism. Gabo's work, a kind of spatial puzzle, involved replacing several of the planes of a cube with interlocking diagonals. The completed stainless-steel work, which is 8 feet high, is an attempt by Gabo to show that "the visual character of space is not angular . . . I enclose the space in one curved continuous surface."

Turn toward the center of the campus now, walking back along Washington Road toward the gym complex. You will cross Prospect Avenue and Ivy Lane (whether you are coming from the Architecture School or Engineering Quad). Just beyond Ivy Lane you'll find your next piece of sculpture within the Fine Hall library (H5), the well-known portrait head of Albert Einstein by the renowned American/British sculptor Jacob Epstein. As you probably know, Einstein was a beloved figure in Princeton for many years, and this tribute to him is appropriately placed in the physics library. Epstein's portrait heads were modeled in clay for casting in bronze and are characterized (as this one is) by many small jagged planes that break up the surface of the work.

In the plaza between Fine Hall and Jadwin Hall (also H5) is another major work in the Princeton collection: Alexander Calder's *Five Disks: One Empty*. Though this giant work is a stabile rather than one of Calder's more familiar mobiles, it nonetheless has the unmistakable Calder style, with its cutouts and circular and pointed forms of black steel and its mood of playfulness. Though originally painted orange (to honor Princeton's traditional colors), the artist blackened the forms after the work was set on the campus in 1971.

Just behind Fine Hall is Jadwin Hall (still H5). Here in the courtyard of the hall is Antoine Pevsner's *Construction in the Third and Fourth Dimension*. Pevsner was the elder brother of Naum Gabo; together they were active in the constructivist movement in Russia in the 1920s. Pevsner's work is also involved with spatial ambiguity. This sculpture, which rises to more than 10 feet, is a bronze abstraction set on a black granite pedestal. It explores the contortion of flat metal planes into shapes that suggest the possibility of infinite continuity.

Cross Washington Road once again and head toward the Computer Science Building (F6), if you are still feeling energetic. (We don't deny that this is a long walk.) Here you will see Michael David Hall's *Mastodon VI*, another contemporary sculpture.

Slightly closer is *Sphere VI* by Arnaldo Pomodoro, an Italian sculptor. You'll find this work in the Butler College courtyard (F5). Pomodoro specialized in negative/positive casting, in which parts of the surface were gouged out, giving his forms an imagery of motion from within. *Sphere VI* is a giant polished bronze with a type of interrupted surface that the artist described as "an expression of interior movement."

If you cross the tennis court area to your left, you'll find yourself at some newer dormitory buildings near the train station. Here is one of the campus's favorite pieces: David Smith's *Cubi XIII*. Situated on the lawn of Spelman Hall (E5), Smith's 9-foot-high stainless-steel sculpture is one of a series of twenty-eight works that he called "Cubi." An exploration of cubist principles in welded steel, these works were designed for outdoor positioning with particular reference to the architecture around them.

Turning back to the heart of the campus, you will pass Dillon Gym and come to Elm Drive. Turn left and walk until you reach a dorm quad called Cuyler. Cross in front of Cuyler to see Prospect Gardens (G3), the college's lovely formal gardens (and a good place for a quick rest). Prospect House, which overlooks the gardens, has a sculpture on its lawn by the American artist Tony Smith called *Moses*.

A strong cubistic work, *Moses* is a painted steel abstraction of angular planes. Smith felt that the parallel uprights suggested the horns of Michelangelo's *Moses* (Moses wears horns because of a misunderstanding by Latinists of the Hebrew word for shining, also the root of the word for horns), and he continued the symbolism. But whether or not you see this geometric work as Moses, you will find it interesting to compare with the other studies in contemporary, angular, hard-edged abstractions on this walk.

You arrive next at the art museum itself (F3). (We expect you will want to return to it after your last few stops.) You can easily identify it by the imposing Picasso in front. *Head of a Woman* is one of those works that is so identified in our minds with Picasso that it hardly needs introduction. Constructed of cast concrete, it was executed by Carl Nesjar (who did many of Picasso's sculptures) from Picasso's maquette of 1962. It was made specifically for this Princeton site, and as it was constructed on campus, students got to watch the process—a unique experience!

Your final stop on the central campus is the courtyard of

Hamilton Hall (E2), back near the gate you originally entered. Here you will find *The Bride* by British sculptor Reg Butler. This tall, slender figure (it stands 7 feet high) is a bronze semiabstract female, whose form suggests something of the shapes of trees and leaves. The work is in the tradition of the British postwar figurative style.

As you leave the campus (don't forget your parking meter!), you may wish to drive to the last two destinations on our sculpture walk. They are both at the Graduate College, which is beyond the golf course to the left of the gate (consult your map). You are headed to A6, where you will want to see Gaston Lachaise's *Floating Figure*, made in 1927. (You may recognize this work from the Museum of Modern Art's Sculpture Garden, where another cast of it is a favorite of sculpture lovers.) A typical example of Lachaise's bronzes, the seated figure balances its rounded forms gently and weightlessly.

Our final destination is to see Kenneth Snelson's *Northwood II*, also in the Graduate College (B6). This is a fitting conclusion to our sculpture walk, for Snelson has become a leading member of the current sculpture stylists. His towering aluminum and steel constructions are supported by cables within the framework. "My concern," he says, "is with nature in its fundamental aspect; the patterns of physical forces in space."

Information: The Princeton University campus is open year-round. For tours and information, call (609) 258–3603; Web site www.princeton.edu.

In the vicinity: Grounds for Sculpture in Hamilton is another site for viewing outdoor sculpture (see chapter 41).

34

Queens' Left Bank: The Noguchi Museum and Socrates Sculpture Park

Long Island City, New York

Directions: To reach the Noguchi Museum from the Queensboro Bridge, take the first right possible (Crescent Street) then another right on 43rd Avenue. Go to the end of 43rd Avenue and take another right on Vernon Boulevard. Turn right off Vernon Boulevard at 33rd Road. The entrance to the museum is on the left at 32-37 Vernon Boulevard. There is easy parking on the street. You can also reach the museum by subway via the N train to Broadway in Queens; walk several blocks (west) toward the Manhattan skyline to Vernon Boulevard. In addition, there is a shuttle bus on weekends that leaves from midtown Manhattan; call (718) 204–7088.

For the Socrates Sculpture Park, from the Queensboro Bridge take the upper level, exit at 21st Street, make a left on Broadway, and go to the intersection of Vernon Boulevard. By subway take the N train to the Broadway stop in Queens and walk 8 blocks along Broadway toward the East River.

Perhaps the most unlikely setting for an artwalk, a truly memorable aesthetic experience is a visit to the changing industrial area of

Long Island City that lies just south of the Queens end of the 59th Street Bridge. Here, amid old warehouses and unidentifiable blocks of buildings, are several wonderful spots to visit only a few blocks from one another. You will find yourself in this neighborhood very quickly after you exit from the Queensboro (59th Street) Bridge, and you may be surprised to discover fine art in this decidedly commercial neighborhood.

The Noguchi Museum and Socrates Sculpture Park quietly existed here for many years, alongside diners and warehouses, but when the Museum of Modern Art and the Museum for African Art moved temporarily to Long Island City, the area became a much more vibrant art destination. New art spaces cropped up, while existing galleries and centers became more visible, making Long Island City especially interesting and amusing to explore.

The Isamu Noguchi Garden Museum on Vernon Boulevard is a veritable shrine devoted to the works of one of the twentieth century's most influential and best-known sculptors. In a setting of careful calm and contemplation, including a sculpture garden filled with Noguchi's characteristic Japanese stone figurations, you can see the evolution of his art, from early figurative pieces to his later stone monoliths. The experience is an introspective one.

In one of the curious juxtapositions of art sites in this multifaceted city, you'll find just blocks away, at the Socrates Sculpture Park, a collection of contemporary sculpture that is truly astounding in its freewheeling originality—some of it good, some fascinating, some quite awful. This most current collection sits on city-owned land on the banks of the East River. The influences of such sculptors as Noguchi—the willingness to leave subject and representation behind in search of other truths—is evident everywhere, though there is nothing among these giant sculptures that vaguely reflects

Noguchi's works themselves. Instead you'll find changing exhibitions of vast and original works, and—of particular interest—the artists themselves can often be seen working at their pieces in this unlikely, weedy field. You may wander at will through the towering constructions, waterside assemblages, and huge forms that are temporarily housed here. While the sculptures at the Noguchi Museum are mostly on permanent display, those at Socrates Park change once or twice a year.

The recently renovated Noguchi Garden Museum is about the best-disguised art center we've discovered on our wanderings through the city. Set into blocks of old warehouses, it appears to be another nondescript rectangular building, but on closer inspection you'll see the angles of a contemporary-style building nestled into its triangular city block. Noguchi wanted a home for his works that would be congenial to their style and to his concept of art's relationship to its surroundings. "These are private sculptures," he said, "a dialogue between myself and the primary matter of the universe."

What you will find at the museum are some 350 works that demonstrate the great Japanese sculptor's spiritual presence, as well as his evolving use of stone and other natural materials. The walled-off sculpture garden brings traditional Asian design to the present. In these delicate stone works, trickling water fountains and abstract shapes and patterns catch the light and give you the sensation of being very far away from both Manhattan and the twenty-first century.

Yet Noguchi was, in fact, a quintessentially contemporary artist. His search was for abstract realities, or what he called "the brilliance of matter" that will turn "stone into the music of the spheres." Everywhere—in the rough stone pillars, the delicate marble pieces, the rounded basalt mounds, the intricate black metal abstractions—you sense the sculptor's preoccupation with pure form and its relationship to the space around it. Under the artist's own direction, the museum has laid out works in a logical progression.

In addition to the sculptures themselves, the museum includes many plans, drawings, and photographs of Noguchi's contributions in other places throughout the world. Among the fascinating examples are a photograph of a marble spiral for children ("to show how the idea of play relates to sculpture"), a dance set designed for Martha Graham ("the stage remained my main testing ground for many years"), and detailed planning drawings of whole city plazas—they are a testament to his continuing interest in sculpture outside the studio. Among the oddities we enjoyed were paper lanterns and a musical weather vane designed by the artist.

But most of all, you will come away with a sense of the artist's serenity and spiritual presence that radiates from these often highly abstract monolithic works. Although this is not art that is easy to understand for the layperson, it is nevertheless an experience that will change the way the most unreceptive observer of contemporary art looks at stone. You will have a new idea of how sculpture can both shape its surroundings and become a part of them.

The transposition to today's environmental sculpture is only a few blocks away. A short walk along Vernon Boulevard and the East River to 31st Street will take you to Socrates Park, New York's largest sculpture park. At first you might think this is an unlikely spot for an important outdoor exhibition space, surrounded as it is by warehouses, industrial buildings, and random vacant lots. But the breathtaking views of Manhattan's skyline directly across the river and the waterfront site proved to be a dramatic setting for the large avant-garde works on display. In these raw, unmanicured four and a half acres, you will probably see the boldest, most original, and certainly most massive sculptures anywhere in the city—from huge steel abstractions piercing the sky to rough-hewn constructions in fantastic configurations, from original structures atop floating barges to waterfront sculptures.

The brainchild of sculptor Mark di Suvero, Socrates Park (which he named in honor of the philosopher who "had a lot to teach" him and in honor of the Greek community in nearby Astoria) was created in the mid-1980s from an eyesore lot filled with heaps of rubble. The idea was to provide a space for large-scale outdoor sculptures where the originality, vision, and creativity of the works were to be considered, rather than the fame of the artists.

Di Suvero was able to lease the property from the city for a nominal fee. From the beginning, the community was encouraged to actively participate in the project to make the park an integral part of its daily life. Local residents, including teenagers, were hired to clean and tend the lot (tons of rubble had to be hauled away) and to be involved in running the park. As the sign at the entrance says, ELEVATION 7 FEET, POPULATION FRIENDLY. And so it is. Socrates Park is a real part of the community, not only used as an exhibition space for outside artists, but also made to be accessible to local would-be artists who may be inspired to add their own unsolicited works to those on display. People come here to walk, to contemplate, to observe, to play.

According to di Suvero, "you're expected to touch the works," much to the delight of the neighborhood children, who can't resist the temptation to occasionally use the place as a wonderful, almost surreal playground. A visitor may be lucky enough to observe artists at work preparing for future shows. In fact, the park's Outdoor Studio program asks its artists to create their sculptures right here on-site over a few weeks' time, during which they are available to discuss their work with the public. On several of our visits we met informally with some of these sculptors and their assistants, all busy at work nailing down massive wood constructions, hauling huge steel parts, or preparing the soil for a future foundation. Chain saws, tractors, and other heavy equipment are often used to produce the massive works and prepare for shows, and neighborhood residents are invited to help in the construction and installation.

There are one or two exhibits annually, each lasting for several months at a time. At each of the park's exhibition openings, you are likely to see performances by musicians, actors, or dancers in and around the sculptures. Some of the works shown have included Robert Stackhouse's *East River Bones*, made from skeletons of sunken ships; Christo Gianakos's *Styx*, a huge double ramp with a platform (perfect for climbing); Jody Pinto's *Watchtower for Hewett's Cove*, a tall wooden structure that looked more likely to be found in the middle of a large field in a Midwest town; Malcolm Cochran's *Scrapyard Temple for Socrates*, whimsical granite pillars around which colorful coffee tins have been attached in drapelike fashion; and Alison Saar's *Fanning the Fire*, resembling a totem pole of wood, tin, and nails on top of which a stern-looking woman is holding a fan. Di Suvero himself (whose waterfront studio is literally next door) often displays his works here.

Information: The Noguchi Museum is located at 32-37 Vernon Boulevard in Long Island City. It is open Wednesday, Thursday, and Friday from 10:00 A.M. to 5:00 P.M. and Saturday and Sunday from 11:00 A.M. to 6:00 P.M. Admission is charged. Call (718) 956–1819 or visit www.noguchi.org.

Socrates Sculpture Park is located at the intersection of Broadway and Vernon Boulevard in Long Island City. It is open seven days a week from 10:00 A.M. until sunset.

There is no admission fee. Call (718) 956–1819 or go to www.socratessculpturepark.org.

In the vicinity: P.S. 1 Contemporary Art Center, at 46-01 21st Street in Long Island City, is an alternative space par excellence housed in a large nineteenth-century brick building that was once a school. Since its renovation in 1976, it has housed working studios as well as galleries for innovative and unusual exhibitions, in addition to some permanent installations. The artists chosen to be in residence come from around the world and usually stay for a year. You can take a tour of the studios to see the artists at work and visit the galleries, where exhibitions change regularly. Permanent displays include James Turrell's *Meeting*, which can be seen daily (except in bad weather), immediately before, during, and after sunset; Alan Saret's *Fifth Solar Chthonic Wall Temple*; and an untitled work by Richard Serra. The gallery is open Wednesday through Sunday from noon to 6:00 P.M. Call (718) 784–2084 for admission fees and reservations, which are necessary for studio tours.

Snug Harbor: Contemporary Art and a Chinese Scholar's Garden

Staten Island, New York

Directions: Staten Island is easily reached by public transportation, but you will need a car if you want to see the many additional sites listed here in one day. Snug Harbor is located on the north shore of the island at Richmond Terrace and Snug Harbor Road, conveniently only 2 miles from the Staten Island Ferry terminal. The Snug Harbor trolley or the S40 bus will get you there.

From Manhattan the best route is by ferry and bus. From Brooklyn, Queens, or Long Island, drive via the Verrazano Narrows Bridge (take Bay Street, with the harbor on your right, to Richmond Terrace at the ferry terminal; Snug Harbor is on your left, after 2 miles). From New Jersey take the Staten Island Expressway (Interstate 278) to the Clove Road/Hyland Boulevard exit; at the traffic light turn left at Clove Road, right at Richmond Terrace, then right at Snug Harbor. For specific auto routes call (718) 448–2500 from 9:00 A.M. to 5:00 P.M. Monday through Friday.

Snug Harbor on the north shore of Staten Island is a find for jaded New Yorkers, art and garden lovers, and anyone else who wants to spend a stretch of time in an unusual and harmonious setting. Originally founded in 1801 as a hospital for retired sailors, its beautiful and expansive grounds and buildings are landmarks. The first of its historic buildings was erected in 1831. There are both large public structures in a variety of architectural styles—ranging from Italianate Revival to Beaux-Arts—and a row of small Gothic Revival houses built to accommodate the tradesmen who served the sailors' home. The grounds include the Staten Island Botanical Garden, an inspiring Chinese Garden, a conservatory, a concert hall, exhibition space, and much, much more.

The buildings are prettily set on an eighty-acre tract of land just across the road from the shoreline and surrounded by a few pieces of contemporary sculpture. Unlike many such cultural centers, Snug Harbor has an informal air. It is a place that has walkways and byways and open doors; its gardens are invitingly simple and its dos and don'ts signs minimal. There are no citylike aspects to Snug Harbor; you might be in a place far removed from the bustle and commerce of New York City when you wander around here. But Snug Harbor is indeed a busy metropolitan center that includes top attractions (like the Metropolitan Opera and Shakespeare in the Park) among its offerings.

As you enter at the main gate (follow signs on Richmond Terrace), you will find yourself on a pathway with the parking lot to your left. Walk through the parking lot to the visitor center in one of the main buildings, where you can pick up a map and other material on the Snug Harbor complex of buildings and gardens.

On leaving the information desk, walk to Chapel Road (directly before you) to Cottage Road to see the wonderful row of five small Victorian cottages. These once housed the baker, gardener, engineer, and farmer who helped to run Snug Harbor in the nineteenth century. Built between 1885 and 1890, the cottages have undergone renovation and are now used for Snug Harbor staff and visiting artists. The road will lead you to Snug Harbor's most impressive recent addition: the New York Chinese Scholar's Garden.

Modeled after the scholar's gardens of the Ming Dynasty (1368–1644), this exquisite one-acre garden is the only outdoor example of its kind in the United States. Its designer (one of China's eminent landscape architects) along with an army of artisans (one hundred in China doing preparatory work on carvings and tiles, and more than forty here) created courtyards, pavilions, a teahouse, and lotus ponds with waterfalls and rocks, reminiscent of the famous Garden for Lingering in Suzhou. And this is indeed a place for lingering. Following the footsteps of fifteenth-century Confucian scholars who strolled about similarly enclosed spaces, you come upon one inviting spot after another bearing such evocative names as the Garden for Dwelling on Poetic Pleasure, the Hall for Listening to Pine, and the Chamber to Rest Head over Glowing Waters, or the Meandering Cloud Wall. (Plaques displaying these and other delightful descriptions are rendered in elegant calligraphy throughout the garden.)

This profoundly beautiful garden takes some time to savor, for there are many intimate spaces and details to discover, from wood carvings, intricate mosaics, and tracery windows in geometric or floral patterns to delicate magnolia blossoms, pruned apricot trees, and bamboos and pines typical of Chinese scroll paintings. The plantings are spare and carefully chosen, and they complement the many stunning stones shaped like exotic sculptures (some 2,500 tons of Tai Lake stone were imported from southern China). Within the garden walls you have a feeling of complete tranquility and separation from the outside world (and the bustling city!) as you contemplate earth and sky or light and shade in the Taoist tradition.

Almost directly across Cottage Road you'll find the Connie Gretz Garden, another of Snug Harbor's many offerings. To reach it you must pass over a moat and through a castlelike structure leading to the formal garden. As you meander through this half-acre maze of intricate pathways and hedges, you eventually reach the walled "secret garden," reminiscent of the one described in the classic novel of the same name. Children of all ages and adults alike will find this spot irresistible.

We now take you to the Staten Island Botanical Garden itself. Retrace your steps back to the cottages along Cottage Road. Opposite them are the greenhouse and the particularly charming flower gardens. The landscape of the entire park is Victorian in feeling, and so are the garden areas. Among the high points of this landscape are the trees, including wonderful willows, and a superb collection of flower gardens.

The Botanical Garden, which moved to the site in 1975, has put in a variety of small gardens: a formal English perennial garden; a butterfly garden (whose plants are specifically nourishing to butterflies); a Victorian rose garden; an herb garden, featuring medicinal and culinary plantings; a "white" garden, which experiments with vertical plantings; a bog garden; and, inside the conservatory, the Neil Vanderbilt Orchid Collection. Any garden enthusiast will enjoy the way these small treasures of plantings are arranged—each (in its own season, of course) is a treat. A variety of tours, lectures, and demonstrations are available, but you can also enjoy wandering on your own.

Of particular charm near the gardens is the Chinese-style pagoda built by Charles Locke Eastlake of England. This little pavilion is a concert site and an additional Victorian touch to the landscape. At the end of the gardens is a dark green latticework enclosure, which we found particularly appealing. It is planted with charming flowers, and you can sit on the white wrought-iron benches and enjoy a summer's day.

You are now in an area called South Meadow. We suggest turning toward the old dark red buildings to the east. These house, among other things, the Staten Island Children's Museum, a cheerful place that features all sorts of hands-on exhibitions for the small fry of the family. There are numerous workshops and events with modest admission charges. Near the museum is an old, charming building known as Veterans' Memorial Hall. This is the site of many concerts, from chamber music to jazz. Built in the style of a nineteenth-century parish chapel, the hall provides an intimate space for small events.

In front of the hall is Chapel Road, once again, and here are the first of the complex's major Greek Revival buildings. These grand, mostly renovated, pale cream buildings house a variety of Snug Harbor's organizations and are both architecturally and historically interesting. There is the Great Hall, the Music Lab, the Art Lab, and, in the next row, the Main Hall. The Art Lab is an art school that also has special presentations of visual art, such as the recent all-island high school show, and solo exhibitions in its Atelier Gallery. The Main Hall's rotunda and ceiling contain renovated murals from 1884; these Victorian-style paintings have Italianate motifs. In the Main Hall you'll find the Newhouse Gallery, one of Snug Harbor's main attractions. The gallery is Staten Island's principal art space and, as such, is an important part of the cultural center.

Adjacent to the Main Hall is a former seamen's dormitory now housing the Noble Maritime Collection. Named after the artist John Noble, this museum and study center features a permanent exhibit celebrating the history and traditions of Snug Harbor. In addition to galleries and exhibitions, there are classes, printmaking workshops, and a library.

Information: The grounds are open year-round seven days a week (except major holidays) from 8:00 A.M. to dusk; they are also open in the evening for occasional special events. Guided tours are offered free, by appointment. The New York Chinese Scholar's Garden is open Tuesday through Sunday from 10:00 A.M. to 5:00 P.M. Admission is charged. Call (718) 448–2500 or visit www.snugharbor.org.

In the vicinity: The Jacques Marchais Center of Tibetan Art (338 Lighthouse Avenue, Richmond; 718–987–3478) is in the most unlikely setting imaginable, on a suburban Staten Island street. In addition to one of the largest private collections of Tibetan art in the country, this unusual center includes a small Tibetan-style garden, artifacts, and musical instruments. Works from other Asian countries are also exhibited in the chock-full, rather small stone buildings, built to resemble a Tibetan monastery.

Siah Armajani's waterfront bridge and tower near the St. George Ferry Terminal is a not-to-be-missed art experience. With this relatively recent (1996) work, Armajani—one of today's leading sculptors of public art—has added real panache to the area. Consisting of a 65-foot-long bridge and a 65-foot-tall tower topped with gold glass in a lighthouse vein, the structure is made of gray wood and steel, with splashes of yellow, orange, and green reminiscent of the sun's rays. From this site you can enjoy spectacular vistas as you walk from the terminal to the plaza, which is still undergoing development. Now somewhat solitary, the esplanade is expected to house art fairs and farmers' markets in the future.

36

De Cordova Sculpture Park: Modern Forms upon a Hill

Lincoln, Massachusetts

Directions: From Boston take Route 128 (Interstate 95) to exit 28B, Trapelo Road/Lincoln. Take Trapelo Road about 2 miles to the intersection with Sandy Pond Road and follow the signs to De Cordova.

The combination of fine modern and contemporary art in an unusually beautiful setting makes the De Cordova Museum and Sculpture Park a remarkable site not to be missed. Situated on the shores of a quiet pond in Lincoln, outside of Boston, its bucolic ambience would be reason enough for a visit: The thirty-five acres of rolling hills, woods, and sweeping lawns with views of the New Hampshire hills create an inviting environment for a walk. But De Cordova also happens to be New England's most important outdoor exhibition space, with more than thirty large-scale sculptures on view.

Once the country estate of Julian De Cordova (1851–1945), an eccentric art-collecting Boston entrepreneur, the property with its odd castlelike structure was given in 1930 to the town of Lincoln.

It was first simply a recreational area, but it gradually evolved into a museum when its potential as an exhibition site was realized. The De Cordova began acquiring and displaying large sculptures by prominent American artists, and since the mid-1980s the complex has included a permanent sculpture park (the only one of its kind in New England) in addition to an indoor museum (housed in what once was De Cordova's mansion) and several other buildings used for classes, studios, and workshops.

Scattered about the spacious grounds—like silent abstract sheep in a pastoral tableau—are modern and contemporary works by a wide variety of American artists. (A map of the grounds and artworks is available at the museum desk.) These range from sculptures by such major artists as Alexander Liberman, George Rickey, and Mark di Suvero to the latest, most innovative environmental pieces. While some works remain at De Cordova as part of its permanent collection (see below), others come and go with the continuous flow of changing exhibits. The sculptures have been carefully placed to interact harmoniously with the beautifully arranged park, creating a landscape that is in itself a sculpted environment.

Although sculptors of national and international stature are well represented here, a large number of artists shown are from New England. De Cordova is considered to be the premier showcase of the region's most promising artists and is committed to generating public appreciation of its local artistic community.

Some of the art has a particular New England focus. Recently a site-specific work by Gail Rothschild called *Women of the 19th Century: A Conversation* was installed in a quiet hemlock grove. Drawn from the writing of a nineteenth-century New England feminist, Margaret Fuller, a transcendentalist colleague of Thoreau and Emerson, it features five giant rocking chairs, each with inscriptions from Fuller and her contemporaries. Placed in each rocking chair is a larger-than-life female figure made of hay held together by chicken wire. The women are kneeling in a way suggestive of the stocks that were used in this region during colonial times. You might draw your own conclusions from this unusual grouping, but the New England context is unmistakable.

Every year De Cordova commissions site-specific works that often speak of environmental issues. A typical show of such work included a sculpture called *Bat House* by Christopher Sproat, built as a real haven for these much maligned creatures. Placed in an open field, the sculpture heralds our need to protect the earth's only flying mammals. The appropriately Gothic-looking, spear-shaped work has a pointed roof and soars 14 feet into the air. It will probably be the only artist-designed bat house you will ever see.

Another unusual installation is Allan Wexler's *Floor Becoming Table on a Hill,* which he located at a leafy site overlooking Flint's Pond. The artist is known for his original—and somewhat eccentric—constructions and arrangements of furniture that reflect the relationships among individuals, architecture, and landscape. This conceptual picnic site includes two 60-foot-long wooden paths that intersect at a junction where people, landscape, art, architecture, and furniture meet and connect. Philosophy and art aside, you can imagine its being a fine place to dine alfresco.

Another artist, Patrick Dougherty, decided to create something that would respond to the castlelike appearance of the museum's building. The result is *Spin-Offs,* an installation in which natural materials have been woven into conical windswept forms that actually appear to move from the top of the turreted structure to the ground.

These sentiments and concerns for the environment find

expression throughout the sculpture park. You may not find all of the specific works mentioned here, since many are not permanently installed. However, the De Cordova has a number of sculptures on its grounds that were gifts to the collection and should be on view at all times. Look for the following: George Rickey's *Three Lines*, a stainless-steel work that focuses on linear movement; Richard Fishman's *Colleoni*, a contemporary bronze homage to Andrea del Verrochio's equestrian monuments; Hugh Townley's intriguing concrete work called *Group of Three*, which spells the word *art* in an abstract manner; Alexander Liberman's *Cardinal Points*, one of the well-known sculptor's abstract welded steel constructions; Ed Shay's *Acadian Gyro*, an intriguing bronze construction that he describes as "a skeletal structure of a fish-boat with winged oars"; George Greenamyer's *Mass Art Vehicle*, a steel construction of a pyramid-shaped vehicle on tracks; Mags Harries's topiary garden constructions that can be seen as "intimate rooms" when viewed from above; Lila Katzen's weathered steel *X Notion Like an H*, which explores the "identity" of the letter X; and Paul Matisse's *The Musical Fence*, made of aluminum sounding bars and concrete, a kind of sculptural vibraphone that stretches to more than 20 feet across the lawn.

The museum's gallery exhibitions sometimes relate to the works in the park. A recent museum show featured thirty plastic models created by Allan Wexler in his investigation of ideas for his picnic area.

The De Cordova is an active, vibrant museum complex with many facilities and activities, including classes, workshops, and visits to artists' studios. Docent tours of the museum and sculpture park are available for those who enjoy discussing art with others as they view the pieces. However, you are welcome to walk around on your own.

Information: The De Cordova Museum and Sculpture Park is located on Sandy Pond Road in Lincoln. The museum is open Tuesday through Friday from 10:00 A.M. to 5:00 P.M. and Saturday and Sunday from noon to 5:00 P.M. The sculpture park is open seven days a week from dawn to dusk. There is an entrance fee for the galleries but not for the sculpture park. Call (617) 259–8355 or visit www.decordova.org.

37

An Inviting Sculpture Park on Corporate Grounds: The Donald M. Kendall Sculpture Gardens at PepsiCo

Purchase, New York

Directions: From New York City take the Hutchinson River Parkway north to exit 28 (Lincoln Avenue). Note the sign indicating SUNY/Purchase. Go left on Lincoln Avenue to its end. Turn right onto Anderson Hill Road; the entrance to the sculpture gardens is on the right.

We have no hesitation in inviting you to take this artwalk; it is truly one of our favorites both with and without children in tow. You may wonder how PepsiCo—so well known for its mainstream popular culture advertising—would find itself in a book about public art and gardens. But you are in for a wonderful surprise. While there are many corporate art collections in America, few are available to the public to enjoy with the scale, variety, and quality of the Donald M. Kendall Sculpture Gardens at PepsiCo.

A walking tour of these 112 acres (more an estate than a

garden in the traditional sense) will introduce you to some forty-two major works of sculpture, as well as to a shining example of how a corporation can enhance its surroundings and bring art to people outside of a museum. The former CEO of the company, Donald M. Kendall, conceived the idea and was active in collecting the sculptures to provide "an environment that encourages creativity and reflects essential qualities of corporate success." (While you may find that few of these works of art seem to relate in any way to corporate success, the sense of creativity is indeed all around you.)

In 1970 Edward Durell Stone's massive headquarters building was opened on this exquisite site, formerly a polo field. The building (which is not open to the public) is made up of seven square blocks that form three courtyard gardens around a central fountain. The architect's son laid out the surrounding acreage of rolling green terrain; there are fields, pathways, a lake, distinctive trees, flower gardens, fountains, and—everywhere you look—sculpture.

The gardens themselves were planned by the internationally known landscape designer Russell Page. Each piece of art is carefully placed in relation to its surroundings so that each knoll or valley provides a gentle setting for its work of art. There are both formal gardens, where smaller pieces of sculpture are surrounded by clipped hedges and precisely groomed plantings, and vast fields, where monumental examples of contemporary sculpture stand starkly against the horizon. There is also a lake and well-tended woodland. This park is so carefully designed and maintained (an army of gardeners seems to be always at work) that even the parking lots are concealed by plantings. You will seldom find this vast place crowded.

To begin your artwalk, leave your car in one of the hidden parking lots (to which discreet signs direct you). After you park, go to the visitor center, pick up a map, and enter the Golden Path, a nice, winding walkway through the entire acreage. (You may wander on your own if you prefer, or stay on the path and follow the map, which identifies all works of art.)

1. As you come to the fork in the path, go to your right. The first sculpture, just to the left of the path, is Alexander Calder's *Hats Off*, a giant work in orange-red metal. Unmistakably a Calder, it is set against a backdrop of white fir and Colorado blue spruce, bringing its brilliant color vividly to life.

2. Also to the left of the path is Jean Dubuffet's painted black-and-white *Kioske Evide*. This 1985 abstract sculpture by the renowned French artist does look like some fantastic kind of kiosk, with its whimsical shapes and painted designs. Dubuffet described his works in this style not as sculptures but as "unleashed graphisms, drawings which extend and expand in space."

3. A little farther, also to your left, is a work by Arnaldo Pomodoro called *Grande Disco*, a variation on the form of the globe, eaten away by some mysterious forces. (Another Pomodoro work—and one of the major sculptures of the entire collection—is described below.)

4. Leave the path and walk left toward the building entrance to see a work by David Smith. This piece, called *Cube Totem Seven and Six*, is set just in front of the trellis to the giant headquarters building. You will no doubt recognize Smith's style in this delightful shiny metal work. (In fact, one of the characteristics of this sculpture collection is that each work is highly typical of its artist's style; if you are familiar with contemporary sculpture, you may enjoy identifying the works without benefit of this guide.)

5 and 6. On the terrace in front of you, you'll find works by two twentieth-century Italian masters. First, you'll see Marino

Marini's charming *Horse and Rider*. Now somewhat of a "classic," Marini's signature horse-and-rider images are familiar but always a pleasure to see anew. Also on the terrace are two Alberto Giacometti sculptures, *Standing Woman I* and *II*, their tall, thin figures sharply defined against the building's wall.

7. Auguste Rodin's *Eve* is perhaps the most traditional work on this artwalk, but it is interesting to see the origins of contemporary sculpture in this lovely 1881 piece. It is charmingly set among holly trees and shrubbery.

8. One of the most interesting works is Max Ernst's *Capricorn*, to the right of the path. Don't miss this surrealistic group of figures with animal parts suggesting fish, a cow, and birds.

(Here is an opportunity to visit the courtyard gardens that contain ten additional works of art. You can either enter the gateway at this juncture or leave them for the end. They are described as numbers 33–42.)

9. One of today's leading sculptors is represented next: In a kind of garden area to your left, you'll find Kenneth Snelson's *Mozart II*. This giant aluminum construction of geometric shapes and wires is a most contemporary tribute to Mozart.

10. Head back to the path and go left at the fork, near the building's walls. Here you'll see George Segal's *Three People on Four Benches*, a characteristically superrealistic work that may remind you of PepsiCo's workers relaxing during their lunch hour break.

11. Claes Oldenburg's *Giant Trowel II* is one of the most memorable sights at PepsiCo. In fact, it is so startling against its background of pine and dogwood trees that you blink to see if the giant spade is really there, digging into the green earth.

12. Moving farther along the path, you'll next see George Rickey's *Double L Eccentric Gyratory II*, a typical Rickey work made up of stainless-steel windmill-like blades that shift gently in the breeze.

13 and 14. Here, on the edge of the cultivated lawn area and in front of a wooded section, you'll come to Tony Smith's abstract *Duck* and Richard Erdman's *Passage*.

15 and 16. David Wynne's *The Dancers* is close to the entrance to the park, near an area called the Stream Garden, as is Art Price's *Birds of Welcome*, a contemporary but rather folksy work that reminded us of Pennsylvania Dutch design.

17–19. Also nearby are *The Search* by Victor Salmones; another David Wynne figure piece, *Dancer with Bird;* and William Crovello's *Katana*. These works are all surrounded by shrubbery and little woodsy walkways, in contrast to those on the terraces or open fields.

20. Some way past these works, to the left of the path, you'll come upon Judith Brown's 1982 *Caryatids*. This is a fascinating post-modern work that is reminiscent of ancient art, using old car parts in a highly contemporary manner. Don't miss this impression of crumbling ruins made of steel bits.

21–23. Gidon Graetz is represented by *Composition in Stainless Steel No. 1*, which you'll find near the building on your left, while *Personnage*, a 1970 work by the "old master" Joan Miró, is up on the terrace near the lily pond. (Don't miss this delightful garden spot with its perennial flower border and water lily pool. Here also is a charming pavilion inspired by eighteenth-century English landscape design; it is a perfect place for a quick rest.) Nearby is Robert Davidson's *Frog*; you'll see a more imposing work by this sculptor later on.

24. Next you'll come to one of the most memorable and defining works in the sculpture park: Arnaldo Pomodoro's *Triad*, a dramatic group of three modern, but ancient-looking, columns set starkly against the landscape.

25 and 26. The well-known British sculptor Barbara Hepworth is also represented in this collection with a typical work. Her *Meridien*, a 1959 piece, is to the left of the path near Bret Price's *Big Scoop*.

27 and 28. Next you'll find the works of two of the most often mentioned sculptors in this book: Isamu Noguchi and Louise Nevelson. Both have defined contemporary sculpture in our time, but in very different ways. Noguchi's *Energy Void* is a characteristically formalistic work; Nevelson's *Celebration II* is a dark collection of geometric metal forms set in soft ground cover amid a stand of copper beech trees that reflect the color of the sculpture.

29. You have now reached the lake. In your walk around it, you'll see several of the major works in the collection. First you'll find Robert Davidson's three giant totems that will remind you of northwest coast Native American carvings. This work, appropriately called *Totems*, stands out with its audacity, bright colors, and dramatic design.

30 and 31. Another contemporary work, Asmundur Sveinsson's *Through the Sound Barrier*, is also next to the circular path around the lake. At the intersection of the lake path and your original entrance to the grounds is one of the park's most beloved sculptures (particularly by children), David Wynne's realistic *Grizzly Bear*.

32. The last work on the grounds is Henry Moore's *Double Oval*, which sits on the edge of the lake as a splendid monument to contemporary art.

33–42. If you haven't already detoured to the courtyards, you may now wish to see the works in the courtyard gardens. These charmingly landscaped collections of plants and art are in the center of the building complex. The majority of the works there are representative of the earlier schools of contemporary sculpture, including two by Henry Moore, two by Henri Laurens, and one by Aristide Maillol. There is also a Seymour Lipton work and David Wynne's *Girl with a Dolphin* in the center of a fountain. Of particular note are the wonderful heavy figures by Laurens, *Le Matin* and *Les Ondines*, which you reach by walking on stones through a watery environment that heightens your appreciation for the art so beautifully placed.

For those of you who enjoy nature as well as sculpture, notice the rare plantings, including some from Japan and China. A list of trees is available at the visitor center, but we want to especially point out the stands of birches and witch hazels, the oak grove, lacebark pine from China, European hornbeam, black locust, sweet gum, walnut, hemlock, cypress, and dawn redwood. Among the wonderful flowering plantings are azaleas, rhododendrons, and crab apples, so you might want to take this walk in April or May, at the height of the flowering shrub season. In any case, we think you'll find this combination of natural and artistic pleasures a rare treat.

Information: The Donald M. Kendall Sculpture Gardens at PepsiCo's headquarters are on Anderson Hill Road in Purchase, New York. The gardens are free and open year-round, seven days a week, from 10:00 A.M. to dusk. Call (914) 253–3000.

In the vicinity: Also in Purchase is the Neuberger Museum at the State University of New York, with modern and contemporary paintings, sculptures, photographs, and prints. Call (914) 251–6133 or visit www.neuberger.org.

Kykuit, the Rockefeller mansion in Pocantico Hills, is set in sumptuous, art-filled grounds; it contains a great collection of twentieth-century art, Chinese ceramics, prints, tapestries, and magnificent outdoor sculptures. See chapter 24 for details.

The Katonah Museum of Art, Route 22 at Jay Street in Katonah (914–232–9555; www.katonahmuseum.org) is an elegant museum featuring loan exhibitions in a most attractive setting.

38

Griffis Sculpture Park: Contemporary Works in a Natural Setting

Ashford Hollow, New York

Directions: From Buffalo take U.S. Highway 219 south to Ashford Hollow. Make a right onto Ahrens Road and go approximately 2.7 miles to County Road 75 (Mill Valley Road). Turn left and go 1.5 miles to the park entrance on the left.

A giant crab, Amazon women, a giraffe, a 28-foot cobra, a reclining nude, a monumental toadstool, and a variety of other astonishing creatures, towers, and constructions dot the grassy landscape of Griffis Sculpture Park. These 400 rolling acres in upstate New York (about 43 miles south of Buffalo) are an appealing art site for the walker and sculpture lover.

You'll find sculptures all over this varied terrain of grassy hills, open meadows, woods, and deep ravines. Some 200 works have been placed at the park for the enjoyment of the art-loving public by the Ashford Hollow Foundation for the Visual and Performing Arts. There are 120 sculptures by Larry Griffis, the CEO of the foundation, and about 80 works by other artists, including Wes Olmstead, Richard Gustin, Julie Siegel, James Suris, Joe Panone, John Bjorge, Frank Toole, Dennis Baraclough, and Roberly Ann Bell, and, surprisingly, the Neighborhood Youth Corps. (The latter created a fountain with an airy design of flying birds.)

As you make your way over 10 miles of hiking trails through this lovely landscape, you'll see art in a wide variety of styles. There are huge steel and iron constructions, traditional marble statues, wood carvings, and sculptures made of a great mix of materials. Among the most interesting works are a collection of oversize human and insect forms and a number of imaginative abstractions that tower over the viewer. A series of 25-foot-tall iron figures with dangling earrings are posted like guards along one road. Called *Ladies in Waiting*, they are designed to "alert and greet visitors," according to Griffis. But you will hardly need alerting at this art site—a visit here will certainly keep you awake!

Griffis had the inspiration for his own sculpture park while picnicking with his family amid the classical ruins of Rome. He envisaged a large parklike setting with trails and meadows for contemporary sculpture instead of ancient ruins. On his return to New York State, he set about making his Roman vision a reality. In 1967 his family purchased the vast acreage of rolling hillside, a foundation was set up, the first of his own works were placed on the grounds, and his sculpture park came into being. Since then it has grown to include works by dozens of other artists in a wide variety of styles.

This is a particularly enticing outing for children, a kind of artistic adventure that is surefire. They can allow free rein to their imaginations, touch the works of art, scamper through the vast fields at will, get lost in a brightly colored wrought-iron maze, and perhaps capture the magic of the collaboration between art and nature that the best sculpture parks create. "Visitors can touch the sculptures, climb on them," says Griffis. "The sculptures become an environment, and the whole park becomes a work too. People are part of the flow here." Periodically, he creates new trails and paths to accommodate the wanderings of both art and nature explorers at the park.

There are musical events at the sculpture park in warm weather. The Ashford Hollow Foundation has provided these acres of art for the pleasure of the public without charge (contributions, however, are gratefully received). The foundation also runs the Essex Arts Center in Buffalo, which houses artists' living and studio spaces, a foundry, and a gallery.

Information: Griffis Sculpture Park is at 6902 Mill Valley Road in Ashford Hollow. It is open daily May through October from dawn to dusk. Tours are available. Call (716) 667–2808 or visit www.griffispark.org.

Two Historic Cemeteries in New York City: Artistic Monuments and Artists' Graves

Green-Wood Cemetery, Brooklyn, New York, and Woodlawn Cemetery, Bronx, New York

Directions: To reach the Green-Wood Cemetery via subway, take the M, R, or N train to 25th Street (Brooklyn); walk up the hill 1 block to the main Green-Wood Cemetery entrance at Fifth Avenue and 25th Street. Call for driving directions and parking information. For Woodlawn Cemetery take the Cross Bronx Expressway to Jerome Avenue. The entrance is on your right, opposite Van Cortlandt Park. You can also take the 4 train or Metro North Harlem Line (from Grand Central) to Woodlawn.

Green-Wood Cemetery is one of the jewels of Brooklyn. Founded by Henry Evelyn Pierpont in 1838, its rolling terrain with flowering trees covers 478 acres. There are vast lawns and four glacial ponds, as well as many serpentine pathways that lead from one site to the next. A treat for bird-watchers, botanists, history buffs, and art lovers, Green-Wood is a must-see destination.

This historic cemetery is the final resting place for notable Americans, from political leaders to Civil War generals to sports figures to artists and writers. In the following walk we guide you to some major sculptural and architectural sites, in addition to the burial monuments of some of the twenty noted artists buried here.

Since many of the specimen trees flower in late spring, this walk is particularly appealing in May, but any time of year is recommended. Pick up a map at the office next to the entrance gate. You can locate some 225 grave sites with its help, but there is a mazelike quality to finding them (it took us hours!), so we have distilled the walk to about 25 comparatively easy-to-find spots. We have used the official map numbers to simplify your walk.

Green-Wood, like many fine cemeteries of its type, is filled with eye-catching mausoleums and statuary. Long before the existence of public parks, people strolled and picnicked in these green acres, and Green-Wood became a Sunday-outing destination. Imitations of historical architectural styles, such as Moorish Revival and classical Greek, are interspersed with dramatic statuary. And great views—including the Statue of Liberty and one where Minerva salutes from the grave of Charles Higgins, creator of India ink—can be had from the many high points in these acres.

Those visitors who enjoy stories of intrigue, romance, and tragedy will find more than enough material here. (For some of these stories, see *Permanently New Yorkers: Final Digs of the Notable and Notorious* by Patricia Brooks, published by the Globe Pequot Press.) We recommend the following walk, with additional detours for those with time and energy to extend the route.

We begin at the wonderful Gothic Revival gates that were designed by architect Richard Upjohn and built between 1861 and 1863. (Upjohn was noted for his church designs in Greek and

Gothic Revival styles, among them Trinity Church in Lower Manhattan.) The entrance gates are marvelous to look at, with their 106-foot-tall central tower, steep slate roofs, cast-iron bannerettes, columns, brilliant sandstone (mined in New Jersey), and four reliefs.

Passing through the gates, we make a left turn onto Battle Avenue. Here, on your right, is our first stop, a memorial to David Stewart (50), coal and steel magnate and father of Isabella Stewart Gardner, Boston philanthropist and museum founder, by Augustus Saint-Gaudens and Stanford White. The reliefs depict two robed angels as musicians.

Continue on to the small Syringa Path, then on to the loop of Bayside Avenue, where three graves are of interest to us. Here Nathaniel Currier (4), the great printmaker, is buried, and in the same circle is the heroic bronze statue honoring DeWitt Clinton (20), a New York governor and senator and father of the Erie Canal. This statue was cast by Henry Kirke Brown, with the base design by Richard Upjohn. Opposite DeWitt Clinton is the (unnumbered) grave called "Little Frankie," carved by Daniel Chester French.

Retrace your steps to Battle Avenue to find a Greek Revival mausoleum with fine Ionic columns honoring John Anderson (38), a mysterious figure in tobacco who was involved in a sensational murder case in the 1840s. Continue on Battle Avenue, past the intersection, for a short distance. On your left is the not-to-be-missed pyramid honoring Albert Parsons (47). Like the Greek Revival temple, the faux-Egyptian pyramid was a popular style in the mid-nineteenth century.

Beyond, you'll come to the intersection with Border Avenue, where you'll find some steps to a scenic lookout and the Soldiers Monument to the New York Troops (98), honoring the city's contribution to the Civil War. If you descend these steps, you'll find two additional Greek Revival mausoleums, the first dedicated to Marcus Daly (26) of Anaconda Copper and the second (at the intersection of Meadow Avenue and Atlantic Avenue) honoring Peter Gilsey (43).

Across the way on Atlantic Avenue is one of the more amusing grave sites, this one dedicated to William H. Beard (106), a nineteenth-century artist noted for his paintings of bears and other animals. Guess what lurks on top of his monument?

Continue some distance on Atlantic, past Grove Avenue. Here a small pathway called Almond Path borders a hillside with many picturesque mausoleums cut into the hill. If you walk around the hill on Grove to Ocean Avenue, you'll find the burial site of the stained-glass maker and painter John La Farge (119). Not far away is the recent grave of contemporary artist Jean-Michel Basquiat (105).

For those with extra stamina, follow Vine Avenue to Sassafras Avenue to see the grave of John Kensett (118), a Hudson River school painter. You can also detour to see a monument of the Biblical Azrael by the American sculptor Solon Borglum (16).

Turn back toward Locust Avenue, follow it to Hazel Path until its intersection with Vernal Avenue, and turn right. Here is a wonderful example of Moorish Revival architecture in the tomb of Commodore Cornelius Garrison (42), a leading industrialist of the mid-1800s.

Continue on Vernal to its intersection with Dale, and turn left to Thorn Path. Here, in a circle, is the burial place of Samuel F. B. Morse (11), artist and inventor of the telegraph. From Thorn Avenue you'll find Orchard Avenue, from which you'll take Amaranth Path to Landscape Avenue. Here is the grave of George Bellows (107), a leading American painter of the early twentieth century. Nearby, again on Orchard Avenue, is an evocative grave showing an empty marble chair, dedicated to one Mary Adsit (13).

Retrace your steps on Orchard to the intersection with Landscape Avenue, which you will take, passing many small paths, to Vista Avenue. Find Crocus Path; here, on a hill, are two interesting grave sites: the impressive open-air church honoring Henry E. Pierrepont (49), the cemetery's founder, and the nearby site dedicated to the American painter William M. Chase (110).

Turning homeward, take Lawn Avenue to its intersection with Landscape Avenue to find the grave of Charles Tiffany (20), founder of Tiffany & Company, as well as that of his son Louis Comfort Tiffany, the noted art-glass designer.

Just across Landscape Avenue on your left is the grave of the leader of the Hudson River painters, Asher B. Durand (112). Also off Landscape Avenue is the grave of another American painter, George Catlin (109), who was unequaled in his depiction of Native Americans. Don't miss the lovely ponds in this vicinity.

Return to Landscape Avenue and turn right into Valley Avenue to find our last grave site of note, which consists of terracotta gargoyles, gables, and evangelists, dedicated to John Matthews (25), the "soda fountain king." (In 1886 this site was celebrated as the "mortuary monument of the year.") This extravaganza is an example of High Victorian style.

Your final stop is Green-Wood's lovely chapel with its pretty stained-glass windows. This early twentieth-century building was patterned on Christopher Wren's Thomas Tower at Christ Church in Oxford and was designed by the architects of Grand Central Terminal.

While we have focused on the arts and architecture, there are numerous grave sites that will appeal to those with other interests. Feel free to explore them at your leisure!

Woodlawn Cemetery comes as a wonderful surprise to the first-time visitor. A peaceful oasis surrounded by a bustling urban environment, it contains a remarkable collection of artistic and historic monuments and mausoleums in an unusually lovely setting. Here, in an idyllic landscape of magnificent trees, shrubs, flowers, and ponds, are buried some 300,000 souls, among them many noted figures in politics, sports, science, industry, and the arts. Their graves range from simple stone markers to grandiose monuments with sculptures, Gothic arches, stained-glass windows, and myriad decorations. To stroll on winding shaded pathways through these vast grounds—about 400 acres of gently rolling terrain—is a rare treat for anyone, especially those who love history, art, architecture, gardens, or even birds (nearly 120 species have been spotted here).

Woodlawn was founded in 1863 as a "rural cemetery," in the tradition of Green-Wood. Like other garden cemeteries it was an inviting spot for leisurely walkers, before urban public parks came into being. The site chosen was within the beautifully wooded Bronx River Valley, which was not yet part of the city at the time but was easily accessible. It soon gained the reputation for being the final resting place of many prominent people, not only from America, but from all around the world.

Since the cemetery now has a greater number of interesting graves than one can possibly see at any given time, we have limited our suggested itinerary to some sites of artistic or architectural importance, as well as to those where noted artists are buried. Our list is by no means comprehensive, and we hope you will make your own discoveries as you zigzag through this labyrinth, searching for the sites.

Before starting off, we recommend that you pick up a map from security, just inside the entrance gates, to help you locate streets. (Note, however, that the numbers in the itinerary below correspond to our choices and not to that of the cemetery.) You'll find the staff unusually helpful, so don't hesitate to ask for directions if you get lost.

Begin by walking to the cemetery's Central Avenue, the wide street directly in front of you at the entrance gates. Our first stop is the Gates Mausoleum (1), a classical Greek temple on the left corner. Here you will note an impressive bronze door with a grieving figure. This is the work of Robert Aitken, a leading American sculptor in the representational style, known for his busts of famous Americans (Thomas Jefferson, Edgar Allan Poe, and Henry Clay, among others).

The Ehret Mausoleum (2) is next, an impressive French-style tomb guarded by stone lions. These creatures protecting George Ehret (a prosperous beer magnate) are by John Massey Rhind, an architectural sculptor who also made commemorative portraits of notable Americans.

Nearby you'll find the Egyptian Revival–style Woolworth Mausoleum (3), a stark white structure featuring two sphinxes. This tomb, where F. W. Woolworth and his granddaughter Barbara Hutton are buried, was designed by John Russell Pope, the architect of the Jefferson Memorial in Washington D.C.; the statues are by the sculptor J. C. Loester.

Continue on Central Avenue, past Park Avenue, to the "Walnut" plots. On your right you'll see the H. A. C. Taylor Mausoleum (4), designed in 1902 by McKim, Mead & White. This is one of eight tombs at Woodlawn by this historically important architectural firm. Next to it are the Leeds Mausoleum (5), designed by John

Russell Pope in 1910, and the Bliss Memorial (6), created by Robert Aitken in 1917, with figures carved by the Piccirilli brothers (one of whom, Attilio Piccirilli, was a sculptor of monuments in his own right).

Cross Central Avenue to Oak Hill. Here you'll find the St. John Memorial of 1916 (7), whose single figure is by noted sculptor William Ordway Partridge. An important creator of commemorative statuary and monuments, Partridge is known for his images of Thomas Jefferson, Alexander Hamilton, Horace Greeley, General Grant (on his horse), Beethoven, and Tennyson, among others.

Just down the road is the Goelet Mausoleum (8), again by McKim, Mead & White. It was once more elaborate, with a gilded front by Edward Sanford. Nearby is the Clark Memorial (9), a grand neoclassical temple decorated with Ionic columns and bas-reliefs by Paul W. Bartlett. This imposing tomb is the final resting place of William A. Clark, a spectacularly wealthy U.S. senator from Montana who, among his many real-estate holdings, owned a lavish 130-room mansion on Manhattan's Fifth Avenue.

Cross Prospect Avenue to the "Hawthorn" plots. Here is the Kinsley Memorial (10) by the legendary sculptor Daniel Chester French, one of the most influential artists of his time. Especially known for his seated Abraham Lincoln at the Lincoln Memorial in Washington D.C., French is well represented across the country, with his many noted war memorials and images of national leaders and allegorical figures. (In New York City you can see several of his works, including the famous *Alma Mater* in front of Low Library at Columbia University.)

Find your way back to Central Avenue and make a left at Lawn Avenue. In this section ("Lake View"), you'll see the imposing Jay Gould Mausoleum (11), where the infamous nineteenth-century financier is buried. Designed in 1884 by H. Q. French, the Greek-style temple with Ionic columns sits majestically on top of a hill, surrounded by enormous weeping beech trees.

Walking left again, following small circular paths, you'll come to the Whitney Family Monument (12), a polished black granite structure designed by Stanford White. This group of grave sites hidden beneath individual shrubs (a custom from the Near East) includes that of the remarkable Gertrude Vanderbilt Whitney. A sculptor, philanthropist, and founder of the Whitney Museum of Art all in one, she created many works that can be seen in various parts of the country, including right here in Woodlawn (see the Untermyer Memorial, stop 18), and abroad.

Nearby, across Observatory Avenue, is our next site, the Warner Mausoleum (13) by noted architect Cass Gilbert. Next, return to Central Avenue and walk to the "Evergreen" plots. On your left will be the Pulitzer Memorial (14), where lie the illustrious newspaperman Joseph Pulitzer (1847–1911) and his family in front of a simple white stone bench. A black bronze figure by William Ordway Partridge (the same sculptor who made the solitary figure in the St. John Memorial, stop 7 above) sits in contemplative mode.

Continue on Central Avenue on your right. In the "Catalpa" section is the grave site of the illustrator James Montgomery Flagg (15). He is perhaps best known for having created the "Uncle Sam Wants You" poster used to recruit soldiers during the two world wars.

Our next stop is farther down Central Avenue and to the left, within the "Magnolia" area. Here you'll come to one of the grandest mausoleums in Woodlawn, the Huntington Memorial (16), an imposing temple of granite and marble, majestically situated above a grand staircase. The enormous bronze door features bas-reliefs by Herbert Adams, known for his architectural figures, war memorials, and allegorical works. Here lie the railroad magnate/robber baron turned philanthropist Collis P. Huntington, his son Archer, and his daughter-in-law, the prominent sculptor Anna Hyatt Huntington, especially noted for her powerful animal and equestrian works. She also sculpted the Arabella Huntington Memorial (commemorating Collis's second wife), which is just to the left of the mausoleum. Surprisingly, it is Anna who is buried here, and not Arabella.

To reach the next stop, you have to take a slight detour, up Ravine Avenue (right) to the intersection with Whitewood Avenue. On your right you'll find the Henry Russell Memorial (17), yet another work by McKim, Mead & White. On your left, off Whitewood, is the aforementioned Untermyer Memorial (18), situated on a beautifully landscaped quarter-acre hillside plot. This garden memorial includes waterfalls, terraces, and a walkway leading to the bronze monument by Gertrude Vanderbilt Whitney. The unusual monument has a middle section open on three sides, like windows with bronze shutters. Fortunately, these are left open so that one can see the three evocative figures inside: a woman with arms stretched upward, a male figure kneeling beside her, and a young woman turning away.

Continue on Whitewood, turn right at Heather, and proceed (again!) to Central Avenue. On your left, within the "Myosotis" area, are several graves to note. The first is the Cronin Memorial (19), called "Memorial to a Marriage," a 2002 work by the sculptor Patricia Cronin. Nearby is the elegant Garvan Mausoleum (20), another classical design by John Russell Pope. This beautiful temple includes columns and a frieze of mourners by the sculptor Edward Sanford. Here lies Francis P. Garvan, a prominent chemist/entrepreneur who helped establish the modern American chemical industry.

The Piccirilli Memorial (21) comes next. Designed by the

most prominent of the six Piccirilli brothers, Attilio, this bronze image of a mother and child is a tribute to the family matriarch buried here. The Piccirilli brothers were noted stone carvers who operated their family sculpture studio right here in the Bronx. They carved stone decorations and sculptures on many public buildings, private mansions, and monuments in the city. Though some of the work was their own design, they also realized the designs of prominent sculptors like Augustus Saint-Gaudens and Frederick MacMonnies.

Nearby, the Straus Family Mausoleum (22), designed by the architect James Gamble Rogers in 1928, includes a funeral barge and commemorates the deaths of Isador and Ida Straus. The couple perished together on the *Titanic*'s fateful journey.

Another longish detour takes you to our next site. Follow Myosotis Avenue and turn left at Alpine. Within this section is the modest stone grave of the artist Walt Kuhn (23), prettily set amid evergreens. Kuhn helped organize the explosive 1913 International Exhibition of Modern Art in New York, which featured works by the French modernists—and to which he personally escorted President Teddy Roosevelt.

Find Alpine again and turn right onto Park Avenue. Here, in the "Oakwood" section, you'll come to the Archipenko Memorial (24), where both the seminal cubist sculptor Alexander Archipenko and his wife, Angelica Bruno-Schmitz (a noted sculptor in her own right), are buried. The work of Archipenko, a leading figure in the history of early modern sculpture, is not represented at this site. Having outlived his wife, he decided to place a sculpture of hers, an abstract seated figure, at their common grave site. (You can see a work by the great master himself later on this tour, at stop 34.)

You are now heading back to the main entrance, to see two

not-to-be-missed mausoleums. The first, on the corner of Tulip and Whitewood Avenues, is the Bache Memorial (25), a very grand tomb, fit for a king—or, in this case, a pharaoh. In fact, Jules Bache, a prosperous stockbroker/collector fascinated with world art, demanded that his architect, John Russell Pope, pattern his final resting place after the Temple of Isis on the Nile River. The result is a large rectangular temple with great columns carved in papyrus motifs and other symbolic decorations. (There are a few other Egyptian-style mausoleums at Woodlawn, though not on as grand a scale.)

The nearby Belmont Mausoleum (26), off West Borden Avenue, is perhaps the most magnificent of all at Woodlawn. And no wonder: It is an authentic replica of the Chapel of St. Hubert at the Chateau d'Amboise in the Loire Valley, originally designed by none other than Leonardo da Vinci! Oliver Hazard Perry Belmont (grandson of Commodore Perry, and a banker who developed Belmont Raceway) and his wife, Alva Belmont (a socialite, once married to William Vanderbilt, and later a suffragette), are buried here. Built by the sons of the famous architect Richard Morris Hunt, this is an elegant structure with exquisite stone spires and carvings depicting the life of Saint Hubert, patron saint of hunting.

Nearby you will find the Borden Lot 6 (27), off Fairview Avenue. A nod to antiquity, this Roman sarcophagus on a pink marble plaza is an example of the work of architects Carriere & Hastings.

You are now near the entrance (and main office), having made quite a circle. If you're still feeling energetic, you can always check out further sites. Following are a few recommendations, among the many worth seeing.

In the "Park View" section (off Park View Avenue), look for

the grandiose Harbeck Mausoleum (28), an unexpected grave that includes its own pipe organ! The structure, designed in 1918 by Theodore Blake from the firm of Carriere & Hastings, is richly decorated with biblical scenes. The Hudnut Memorial (29), commemorating perfume manufacturer Richard Hudnut, is by sculptor Alexander Zeitlen.

The graceful Irene and Vernon Castle Memorial (30) commemorates this famous early twentieth-century dance team with an evocative sculpture by Sally Farnham, a protégé of Frederic Remington. Though mostly known for her images of western themes and horses, the artist here depicts a dancer, tired after a long day. *The End of the Day* also includes a graceful group of columns surrounding the seated figure.

Take Hickory to Filbert to the Mori Memorial (31), in the "Clover" section. The figure in this 1927 memorial (designed by Raymond Hood) is the work of the illustrious sculptor Charles Keck. A student of both Philip Martiny and Augustus Saint-Gaudens (with whom he later collaborated), Keck is especially known for his commemorative portraits of Lincoln, among other notable Americans.

The Joseph Stella Mausoleum (32), off West Border Avenue, commemorates the Italian-born artist who painted skyscrapers, bridges (his image of the Brooklyn Bridge has become an American icon), and other New York scenes.

From West Border take Filbert then Hickory to the "Goldenrod" area. The two sites not to miss here are the Harkness Mausoleum (33) and the Romney Memorial (34). The Harkness grave site is one of our favorite spots in the cemetery. This unusually lovely setting includes a little stone chapel (designed by the architect James Gamble Rogers) and—of special interest to garden lovers—an intimate walled garden designed by the formidable landscape architect Beatrix Jones Ferrand. You will want to linger at this inviting place! Nearby is the Romney Memorial, which features a big bronze pot by Alexander Archipenko.

The last two sites on our walk are the graves of Josef Stransky (35) and Thomas Nast (36). Walk along Filbert Avenue and turn right at North Border. In the "Rose Hill" section, on your right, you'll see the grave of Stransky, a composer who conducted the New York Philharmonic from 1911 to 1923. What distinguishes this plot is that the gravestone is another work of Attilio Piccirilli. (As of this writing, the music reproduced on the stone is being researched.) To reach Nast's grave site, continue on North Border and turn right on Birch Avenue; look for the marker on your right. Nast, the influential nineteenth-century illustrator and cartoonist, created the popular Santa Claus image, the donkey and elephant symbols for the Democratic and Republican parties, and many other political cartoons. His tomb is one of the most modest to be found at Woodlawn.

Information: Green-Wood Cemetery is located at Fifth Avenue and 25th Street (500 25th Street) in Brooklyn. The main entrance is open daily from 8:00 A.M. to 5:00 P.M. (7:00 A.M. to 7:00 P.M. Memorial Day weekend through Labor Day), weather permitting. Call (718) 768–7300 or visit www.green-wood.com.

Woodlawn Cemetery is located at Webster Avenue and East 233rd Street in the Bronx. It is open daily from 8:30 A.M. to 5:00 P.M. Call (718) 920–0500 or visit www.thewoodlawncemetery.org.

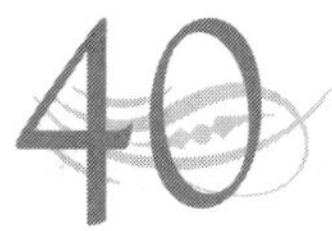

Spectacular Sculpture and Scenery at Storm King Art Center

Mountainville, New York

Directions: From New York City take the George Washington Bridge to the Palisades Interstate Parkway north to the New York State Thruway. Take exit 16 (Harriman) to Route 32 north. Go about 10 miles and follow the signs to Storm King Art Center.

If you have never been to Storm King Art Center in Mountainville, New York, you can look forward to an extraordinary experience. If you have already been there, it is surely time to go back. For this great museum can be enjoyed again and again, with new discoveries to be made on each visit.

Storm King is one of the most important and impressive outdoor sculpture parks in the country. You are struck by the sheer drama and scope of the site the minute you enter through the stone gates. Large, compelling sculptures—many in brilliant primary colors—suddenly appear before you like enormous creatures, in striking contrast to the gently rolling hills and vast grassy fields of the surrounding Hudson Valley. It would be hard to find another place where outdoor sculpture it so dramatically exhibited.

The 400-acre park includes more than 200 modern sculptures—some of truly massive proportions and fantastic shapes—imaginatively set throughout the spacious grounds. Mostly made of metal or stone, these abstract forms range from the smaller, more delicate works on display in and around the manor house to the boldest of sculptures beyond. You can walk on grassy slopes, wooded paths, and fields from one work to another to view each piece up close, or stand on top of one of the hills and admire them from afar. The combination of first-rate art and extraordinary spaciousness makes Storm King unique.

This great property once belonged to a lawyer named Vermont Hatch, who built the elegant Normandy-style stone mansion that is now used to show temporary exhibits and smaller works from the permanent collection. But it was his neighbor and friend, Ted Ogden, an energetic and visionary entrepreneur and art collector, who had the imagination to convert the estate into a sculpture museum. He had seen photographs of Henry Moore sculptures set on a sheep ranch in Scotland and thought Storm King would lend itself to display contemporary art in an even more inspiring way. In a bold move Ogden acquired fourteen David Smith sculptures all at once, and they became the core of the collection. (These sculptures can now be seen on the grounds near the house as well as inside.)

He gradually added pieces by other well-known artists such as Alexander Calder, Mark di Suvero, Louise Nevelson, Robert Grosvenor, Barbara Hepworth, Henry Moore, and Charles Ginnever, to name a few. Since Ogden's death in 1974, many more have been added to what was an already impressive collection, including works by lesser-known contemporary artists, or what are now known as "emerging artists." To accommodate this large body of works—some of which are monumental in size—it has been necessary to clear more land and to create hills and paths. Today's Storm King is still in the process of evolution and expansion; it is an ever-changing landscape.

You will find Storm King a wonderfully inspiring place to walk and contemplate art and nature at your own pace and leisure. There are daily one-hour guided tours that are informative and interesting. However, we preferred seeing the center on our own, roaming freely from one spot to the next. The walk can be a very long one indeed if you are determined to examine each piece of sculpture; you can cover miles, climbing up and down hills and treading through broad fields. Or you can choose to see a selection of works that particularly interest you, reserving the others for a future visit, or perhaps view some of the works from a distance.

The quality of Storm King's art in combination with its unique environment makes it special to a wide variety of visitors, including foreign tourists who relish this taste of the vast American panorama. It is also a perfect place to introduce children to contemporary sculpture. Here they can experience fine art without the usual museum restrictions and can enjoy running about in the grass, from one piece to the next.

Although, in principle, visitors are not allowed to touch the sculptures, there are two notable exceptions: Siah Armajani's *Gazebo for Two Anarchists: Gabriella Antolini and Alberto Antolini* and Isamu Noguchi's *Momo Taro*. The latter is an impressive forty-ton granite sculpture that was created with the idea that people would sit in it. You will often see family groups crowded inside its inviting hollows, posing for a photo scene that would undoubtedly please the artist. Considered to be one of Noguchi's major works, *Momo Taro* sits on a small hill that was especially created to accommodate the work.

And now for the actual walk. After you have reached Storm King, paid your entrance fee, and collected your visitor's map at the gate, you will drive along a beautiful allée graced by tall trees, catching your first glimpse of the enormous abstractions that punctuate the landscape on either side. Park your car near the museum center and walk inside, if you wish, to see exhibits within and to collect whatever literature you may find of interest. Note that each piece of sculpture at Storm King is clearly labeled on-site, so you may not need an elaborate guidebook in addition to your map. Perhaps you will be impatient to set out at once to see the outdoor exhibits, reserving the interior ones for later.

The grounds closest to the house include semiformal gardens with relatively small sculptures tastefully set around shrubbery, planted areas, and walkways. An unmistakable Louise Nevelson black abstract construction called *City on the High Mountain* is located near the entrance, and a brilliant orange Alexander Calder stabile, *Sandy's Butterfly*, is just beyond. (There is an entire hillside of Calders on the other side of the house; his bold 56-foot-high work, *The Arch*, a dramatic black steel construction reminiscent of a prehistoric creature, is close to the entrance of the park. This artist is certainly well represented at Storm King!)

Near the manor house are fairly representational works by such artists as Emilio Greco and Henri Etienne-Martin, all set within view of a striking group of Ionic columns. These columns—brought here from nearby Danskammer, a Hudson River estate that was dismantled some time ago—add to the idyllic setting but are not considered part of the art exhibit.

From here you look over a vast valley accented by a number of bold works. Among these are Mark di Suvero's monumental

Mother Peace and *Mon Pere, Mon Pere* and Alice Aycock's stunning *Three Fold Manifestations II*. To walk to some of these sculptures will take some stamina. Near the columns is an area that is reserved for annual temporary exhibits. Especially interesting recent shows featured the works of Ursula Von Rydingsvard and Siah Armajani. Just beyond is a grouping of eight of the original series of David Smith sculptures overlooking the Calder stabiles mentioned above. These delicate and subtle works are in sharp contrast to much of the sculpture at Storm King.

As you move away from the house, the landscaping becomes more open and the sculptures larger and more daring. Don't miss the naturalistic grouping of stone *Spheres* by Grace Knowlton, tastefully set on a hillside near a clump of trees. A casual observer might think of them as part of the landscape, a tribute to the artist's ability to integrate them into the environment, in much the same spirit as the works of Noguchi. In sharp contrast is Kenneth Snelson's gracefully contrapuntal geometric work in brilliant metal called *Free Ride Home*.

To see Noguchi's *Momo Taro*—certainly one of the most popular works at Storm King—you must walk up a knoll to its commanding site. The breathtaking view from here takes in a stunning group of works. Directly in front of you is Menashe Kadishman's *Suspended*, a massive steel suspension that seems to defy all the laws of gravity. (You will be unable to resist going up to test it.) On your left, piercing the sky above the trees, is Tal Streeter's bright orange *Endless Column*, an original metal zigzag. You'll also see Alexander Liberman's massive steel structures in bright primary colors and deep browns, *Ascent, Eve, and Adonai*, in addition to many other works.

If you walk down the hill, then up again and proceed left, you'll find a wooded path that will take you to a newer area where smaller, more naturalistic stone pieces have recently been placed.

Undoubtedly, there will be new discoveries to be made on each visit to Storm King. We recommend bringing a picnic lunch on your visit: There are few restaurants in the vicinity, and a charming picnic spot with tables (in a grassy area near the lower parking lot) awaits you.

Information: Storm King is open April through November, every day except Tuesday, from 11:00 A.M. to 5:30 P.M. Because of its vastness, it never seems crowded, so you should not fear coming on weekends. Free walking tours are offered daily at 2:00 P.M.; reservations are not required. Admission fees are moderate. Call (845) 534–3115 or 534–3190 or visit www.stormking.org.

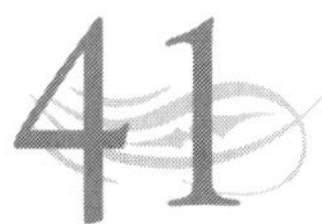

Grounds for Sculpture: Fairgrounds Turned Art Site

Hamilton, New Jersey

Directions: Take the New Jersey Turnpike to exit 7A, then Interstate 195 west to Interstate 295 north. Take exit 65B (Sloan Avenue west), go 0.2 mile, and turn right at the first traffic light. Following the Grounds for Sculpture signs, turn left onto Klockner Road, then turn right at the first traffic light. After traveling less than a mile, make the second left turn onto Sculptors Way. Go 0.2 mile and turn left onto Fairgrounds Road; you'll find Grounds for Sculpture down the road a bit, on your right.

Grounds for Sculpture is a relatively new (it opened in the early 1990s) sculpture park and museum situated in Hamilton, on the former site of the New Jersey State Fair. The twenty-two acres of sloping terrain (once quite flat, like most of the region) are dotted with about 170 contemporary works set in an arboretum-like landscape of crab apples, dogwoods, weeping beeches, conifers, and other specimen trees. The grounds also contain a serene lotus pond, woodland marshes, a gazebo with observation deck (where you can have a snack and enjoy the view), and a picturesque iron arbor (a remnant of the past) with wisteria. Two large glass-walled museum buildings house the more intimate artworks and changing exhibitions, and provide dramatic views of the outdoor installations.

The often bold, contemporary outdoor pieces are placed carefully in harmony with their natural surroundings, as well as amid the impeccably groomed flowering trees and shrubs. The works displayed are by both established and emerging artists, American and international, and they vary in size from monumental to very small indeed. Unlike the sculptures found on the nearby Princeton campus (see chapter 33), these are likely to be by avant-garde artists whose names may not be familiar. Although some installations are permanent, there are temporary displays (usually three changing exhibits a year).

Grounds for Sculpture was created by the well-known sculptor J. Seward Johnson Jr., whose works are well represented elsewhere in the area (including in Princeton). His especially witty (and typically realistic) *Dejeuner Deja Vu*, a takeoff of Édouard Manet's seminal painting *Dejeuner sur l'Herbe*, is on permanent display here. You'll find his lifelike figures seated quietly in the woods, on the edge of a small secluded pond.

The park provides a striking setting for viewing art and nature together. On the grounds you'll find nice benches for resting, as well as an elegant restaurant with a terrace overlooking the scenic gardens.

Information: Grounds for Sculpture is located at 18 Fairgrounds Road in Hamilton. It is open Friday, Saturday, and Sunday from 10:00 A.M. to 4:00 P.M. and by appointment Tuesday, Wednesday, and Thursday from 9:00 A.M. to 4:00 P.M. Admission is free. Call (609) 586–0616 or visit www.groundsforsculpture.org.

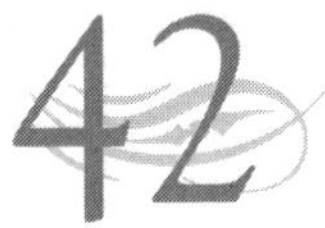

José Clemente Orozco: A Master's Murals at Dartmouth College

Hanover, New Hampshire

Directions: From Boston take Interstate 93 to Interstate 89 to Interstate 91 north. Dartmouth College is north of Lebanon, New Hampshire.

Hanover, New Hampshire, may seem an unlikely place to find a series of brilliant wall paintings by a major Mexican painter. But here, amid the ivy-covered buildings, white frame houses, and quintessential New England campus setting of Dartmouth College, you can see the impressive 3,000-square-foot mural *An Epic of American Civilization* by the twentieth-century master muralist José Clemente Orozco.

Orozco was commissioned in 1932 to paint murals for Baker Library, one of the central buildings on the Dartmouth College campus. These vibrant frescoes are a riveting depiction of some 5,000 years of Latin American life, beginning with the Mayan and Toltec civilizations. (It should be kept in mind that Dartmouth has always had a particular interest in indigenous peoples; its eighteenth-century charter stipulated that Native Americans should be among its students.)

A native of Mexico, Orozco established a monumental and expressive style in his murals, using subjects drawn from Mexican history and other political events. The plight of the native peoples of Mexico under the yoke of the conquistadores, and Latin American revolution, were themes that reappeared in many of his murals.

Orozco was one of several Mexican artists in the twentieth century who turned to a contemporary style of fresco painting to express profound humanist and political beliefs. Combining their own pre-Columbian artistic heritage with a modern European sensibility, these painters revitalized an art form that had been in large part dormant for centuries.

Following the Mexican Revolution and the subsequent decades of political upheaval, these artists first became prominent in the 1920s and '30s. Using their own styles of expressionism and pre-Columbian forms and images, they found a way, through mural painting in public buildings, to bring their artistic and political messages to the people. Major murals by Diego Rivera, David Alfaro Siquieros, and Orozco can be seen in public spaces in many parts of the Western Hemisphere.

In 1932, after a trip to Europe where he saw some of the greatest European frescoes, including the ancient wall paintings of Pompeii, Orozco began the series of murals on the walls of Baker Library. For two years he worked on these dramatic paintings, bringing to the austere New England campus a brilliant taste of his political views and emotional style.

The murals at Baker Library, considered among the major murals in the United States, represent the history of Mexico as a parable for the destruction of humanity. They depict the ancient indigenous world of Mexico under Quetzalcoatl, the conquest by

Cortes, the rise of science and mechanism, and Christ the avenger, who destroys his own cross as civilizations fall.

You can visit the library (identifiable by its 200-foot tower) at any time the college is in session, including summer, and there is no admission fee. For more information about the murals, you can listen to a descriptive telephone recording available at the reserve book desk in the library.

There are several other notable works of art on the Dartmouth campus. Just outside Sanborn Library you'll find Mark di Suvero's metal and wood abstraction called *Chi Delta*.

Beverly Pepper's outdoor sculpture, *Thel*, is a triangular steel work that can be seen on the lawn of the Fairchild Science Center; the artist intended its white panels to disappear under the snow in winter and to emerge anew in the spring.

Inside the Hopkins Center there are three galleries that present a variety of exhibitions from the college collections and other sources, and in Wilson Hall you'll find an anthropological museum that features pre-Columbian North American arts and crafts—an interesting counterpoint to the Orozco murals. The Dartmouth College Museum and Galleries in Carpenter Hall has an impressive collection of Greek and Russian icons and some monumental Assyrian reliefs from the sixth century B.C.

Information: A map and guide to many other sites of interest can be obtained at the college's information desk. This is a beautiful campus with many historic buildings; we recommend planning to spend some time here. Tours of the campus are available. The telephone number for general information is (603) 646–3278; Baker Library (603) 646–2560. The Web address is www.dartmouth.edu.

In the vicinity: Dartmouth College is a short distance north of Aspet, the Saint-Gaudens house and studio in Cornish, New Hampshire (see chapter 28). The Montshire Science Museum (802–649–2200) in nearby Norwich, Vermont, has a kinetic sculpture (created by Fred Crusade) that can be operated by viewers.

Choosing an Outing

Nineteenth-Century Americana

Artists' views of the Hudson Highlands at West Point, 1
A vision of Storm King Mountain, 2
Fitz Hugh Lane in Gloucester, 4
The Hudson River artists at Kaaterskill Falls, 5
Starrucca Viaduct, 6
William Sidney Mount, genre painter, 10
Jasper Cropsey, Hudson River school painter, 24
Daniel Chester French's Chesterwood, 26
Homes of Thomas Cole and Frederick Church, 27
Augustus Saint-Gaudens's Aspet, 28
Samuel F. B. Morse's Locust Grove, 30
West Laurel Hill Cemetery, 32

American Impressionism

Maine islands and Childe Hassam, 7
An impressionists' boardinghouse in Old Lyme, 25
J. Alden Weir and Weir Farm, 29

Early Modernism

Modernists at Lake George, 3
John Marin in Maine, 7
Cape Cod's art colony, 9
Princeton's campus sculpture, 33
Sculpture at PepsiCo, 37
Masterworks at Storm King, 40
José Clemente Orozco at Dartmouth, 42

Contemporary Styles

Cape Cod's art colony, 9
Creative Glass, 11
Monument to the coal miners, 15
Bluestone environmental sculpture, 18
East Hampton's art scene, 31
Princeton's campus sculpture, 33
Noguchi Museum, 34
Socrates Sculpture Park, 34
A countryside sculpture garden, 36
Sculpture wonders at PepsiCo, 37
Outdoor art in a rustic setting, 38
Masterworks at Storm King, 40
New Jersey sculpture park, 41

Environmental Art

Monument to the coal miners, 15
Bluestone environmental sculpture, 18
Animal kingdom in plant forms, 16 and 23
Topiary garden art, 16 and 23

Sculpture Parks and Outdoor Art

Elegance on Long Island, 14

The delights of trompe l'oeil, 17
Bluestone environmental sculpture, 18
Daniel Chester French's Chesterwood, 26
Augustus Saint-Gaudens's Aspet, 28
Princeton's campus sculpture, 33
Noguchi Museum, 34
Socrates Sculpture Park, 34
Sculpture in Snug Harbor, 35
Countryside sculpture garden, 36
Sculptural wonders at PepsiCo, 37
Outdoor art in a rustic setting, 38
Masterworks at Storm King, 40

Artistic Gardens

A Maine island garden, 7
Elegance on Long Island, 14
Plant sculpture in eccentric forms, 16 and 23
The delights of trompe l'oeil, 17
Gardens of Chinese landscape painting, 20 and 35
Impressionist paintings brought to life, 21
Twentieth-century design at Manitoga, 24
Augustus Saint-Gaudens's Aspet, 28

Walks through the Landscape: Inspiring Vistas of Land and Sea

Views of the Hudson Highlands at West Point, 1
A vision of Storm King Mountain, 2
Modernists' views of New York, 3
Fitz Hugh Lane and the northeast seacoast, 4
Kaaterskill Falls, 5
The picturesque Susquehanna Valley, 6
Maine's offshore art colonies, 7
The Grandma Moses landscape, 8
Cape Cod's mecca for artists, 9
Trompe l'oeil in rural New York, 17
Neoclassical tradition at Untermyer Park, 19
Gardens of Chinese landscape, 20 and 35
Bucolic pleasures and river views in Connecticut, 25
A sculptor's estate in the Berkshires, 26
The New Hampshire estate of Augustus Saint-Gaudens, 28
Stone walls and apple trees at Weir Farm, 29
Planned landscape delights at PepsiCo, 37
Outdoor art in a rustic setting, 38
Hills, vistas, and sculpture at Storm King, 40

Distinctive Houses with Artistic Interest

Elegance on Long Island, 14
Estate in Maryland "hunt country," 16
Murals and objets d'art at Wethersfield, 17
Russel Wright's Manitoga, 24

Houses of Hudson River artists, 24 and 27
Impressionists' boardinghouse in Old Lyme, 25
Home and studio of Daniel Chester French, 26
House and elegant studios of Augustus Saint-Gaudens, 28
Home and rustic studios of J. Alden Weir, 29
Samuel F. B. Morse's Locust Grove, 30
Pollock-Krasner house and studio, 31

Monuments of Note

Fort Putnam at West Point, 1
Starrucca Viaduct, 6
Monument to the coal miners, 15
Neoclassical tradition along the Hudson, 19
Pyramids, Gothic arches, and classical temples, 32
New York City's historic cemeteries, 39

Arts and Crafts

Wheaton Village Glass Factory, 11
Peters Valley, 12
Sugar Loaf, 13

Index of Artists, Architects, and Selected Art Sites

Abingdon Art Center, 169
Adams, Herbert, 217
Adams Memorial, 135
Aitken, Robert, 215, 216
Aldrich Museum of Contemporary Art, 147
American Precision Museum, 141
Annigoni, Pietro, 82
Appledore Island, 31–34, 37, 38
Archipenko, Alexander, 219, 222
Armajani, Siah, 192, 225, 227
Aspet, 127, 133–40, 234
Avery, Milton, 16, 47, 48
Aycock, Alice, 227

Babb, George, 137
Bacon, Henry, 124
Baker Library, 233
Baraclough, Dennis, 207
Bartlett, Paul W., 216
Basquiat, Jean-Michel, 212
Beard, William H., 212
Beck, Walter and Marion, 91–92
Belcher, Samuel, 118
Bell, Roberly Ann, 207
Bellows Falls, 141
Bellows, George, 36, 212
Benjamin, Asher, 141
Bennington Museum, 40, 43
Bjorge, John, 207
Blake, Theodore, 221
Bohm, Max, 47
Bolton Landing, 14
Borglum, Solon, 212
Bosworth, William Welles, 88, 107
Brooks, James, 153
Brown, Judith, 202
Brown, Henry Kirke, 211
Browne, Matilda, 116
Bruno-Schmitz, Angelica, 219
Brush, George de Forest, 136
Bush-Holley House, 120
Butcher Sculpture Garden, 170
Butler, Reg, 179
Butler, Robert, 127
Butler Sculpture Park, 127

Caillebotte, Gustave, 97
Calder, Alexander, 168, 174, 177, 200, 224, 226, 227
Calder, Alexander Milne, 168
Calder, Alexander Stirling, 168
Cape Ann Historical Association, 17, 19
Carreiro, Joseph, 103
Casilear, John W., 13–14
Cassatt, Mary, 82
Catlin, George, 213
Cedaridge Garden, 95–98
Cézanne, Paul, 95, 96, 97
Chadwick, William, 115, 116
Chagall, Marc, 106, 108
Chase, William Merritt, 115, 152, 213
Chester, Daniel, 127, 216
Chesterwood, 122–27
Church, Frederick Edwin, 128–29, 130–32
Cochran, Malcolm, 185
Cohen, Lewis, 115
Cole, Thomas, 21, 22, 25, 27, 128–30
Collins, Lester, 92–93
Colman, Samuel, 9–11
Connie Gretz Garden, 190
Cos Cob, 120–21, 145, 147
Cox, Lucia, 152
Crawley, George, 72
Cresson, Margaret French, 125

Cronin, Patricia, 218
Cropsey, Jasper, 8, 26, 27, 28–30, 90, 105–7, 109, 150
Crovello, William, 202
Crusade, Fred, 234
Cunningham, Linda, 170

Dartmouth College, 140, 231–33
Dash, Robert, 99–101
Davidson, Robert, 47, 202, 203
Davis, Stuart, 16
De Cordova Museum and Sculpture Park, 193–97
Deer Isle, 34–35, 38
Degas, Édouard, 82
de Kooning, Elaine, 152
de Kooning, Willem, 152
Delaware Water Gap National Recreation Area, 61, 65
Deming, Thomas, 136
DIA Beacon, 150
Dickinson, Edwin, 47
di Suvero, Mark, 184–85, 194, 224, 226–27, 233
Donald M. Kendall Sculpture Gardens, 198–204
Donatello, 135
Dougherty, Patrick, 195
Doughty, Thomas, 6–7
Dubuffet, Jean, 200
DuMond, Frank Vincent, 113
Dunlap, William, 22
Durand, Asher B., 10, 22, 213

Eagle Bridge, 39–43
Eastlake, Charles Locke, 190
Engman, Robert, 170
Epstein, Jacob, 176
Erdman, Richard, 202
Ernst, Max, 152, 201
Etienne-Martin, Henri, 226

Farnham, Sally, 221
Ferrand, Beatrix Jones, 222
First Congregational Church, Old Lyme, 117, 118, 120
Fishman, Richard, 196
Fite, Harvey, 84–86
Flack, Audrey, 153
Flagg, James Montgomery, 217
Flannagan, John, 82
Florence Griswold Museum, 114–20
Foote, Will Howe, 116
Fort Putnam, 4–5
Francis, Sam, 47
Frankenthaler, Helen, 47
Fraser, James Earle, 136
Frelinghuysen, Suzy, 127
French, Daniel Chester, 122–27, 141, 211, 216
French, H. Q., 217
Frostburg State University, 74–76

Gabo, Naum, 176, 177
Giacometti, Alberto, 107, 201
Gianakos, Christo, 185
Gifford, Sanford, 22
Gilbert, Cass, 217
Gilbert Stuart Birthplace, 104
Ginnever, Charles, 224
Gottlieb, Adolph, 47
Graetz, Gidon, 202
Grandma Moses. *See* Robertson, Anna Mary
Greacen, Edmund W., 116
Greber, Jacques, 72
Greco, Emilio, 226
Greenamyer, George, 196
Green Animals, 79, 102–4
Green-Wood Cemetery, 209–13, 222
Griffin, Walter, 115
Griffis, Larry, 207–8
Griffis Sculpture Park, 206–8
Gross, Chaim, 47
Grosvenor, Robert, 224
Grounds for Sculpture, 179, 229–30
Guild Hall, 152, 153, 154
Gustin, Richard, 207

Hadany, Israel, 170
Hall, Michael David, 177
Hammond Museum, 18–19
Hancock Shaker Village, 126
Hare, David, 152
Harries, Mags, 196
Hartley, Marsden, 34
Hassam, Childe, 32, 33, 115–16, 117, 121, 143, 152, 153
Havell, Robert Jr., 5
Hawkins-Mount Homestead, 50, 53
Hawthorne, Charles W., 46, 48
Henri, Robert, 36
Hepworth, Barbara, 203, 224
Hoffman, Hans, 47
Homer, Winslow, 36
Hood, Raymond, 221
Hopper, Edward, 36, 47, 48
Hozhauer, Emil, 36
Hudson River Museum, 90
Hunt, William Morris, 32
Huntington, Anna Hyatt, 218
Hyde Collection, 14–15

Ingres, Jean Auguste, 82
Inness, George, 65
Innisfree Garden, 83, 91–93
Iselin, Louis, 139

Jacques Marchais Center of Tibetan Art, 192
Jasper Cropsey Studio, 106–7, 150
Jimmy Ernst Artists' Alliance, 152
Johnson, J. Seward, Jr., 230
Jongers, Alphonse, 115

Kaaterskill Clove, 22
Kaaterskill Falls, 8, 11, 20–27, 132
Kadishman, Menashe, 227
Kandell, Victor, 47
Katonah Museum of Art, 205
Katzen, Lila, 147, 196
Keck, Charles, 221
Kensett, John Frederick, 4, 212
Kent, Rockwell, 36
Kline, Franz, 47
Knaths, Karl, 47
Knowlton, Grace, 227
Kosciuszko Garden, 7
Kosciuszko Monument, 6–7,
Krasner, Lee, 151–54
Kuhn, Walt, 219
Kykuit, 106, 107–8, 204

Lachaise, Gaston, 179
Ladew, Harvey Smith, 77–79
Ladew Topiary Gardens, 77–79, 104
La Farge, John, 135, 212
Lake George, 12–14
Lane, Fitz Hugh, 16–18
Laurens, Henri, 204
Layland, Charles, 170
Léger, Fernand, 152
Leicester, Andrew, 74–76
LeWitt, Sol, 147
Liberman, Alexander, 147, 194, 196, 227
Lincoln Memorial, 123, 124, 216
Lipchitz, Jacques, 172, 174
Lipton, Seymour, 204
Locust Grove, 148–49
Loester, J. C., 215
Long Island Museum of American Art, History & Carriages, 53
Lutz, Winifred, 170
Lyme Art Association, 117, 119
Lyme Historical Society, 117–18

MacMonnies, Frederick, 136, 219
Madison Square (Admiral Farragut statue), 135
Madoo, 99–101
Magritte, René, 81
Maillol, Aristide, 204
Manet, Édouard, 230
Manitoga/Russel Wright Center, 106, 109
Manship, Paul, 89

Margo, Boris, 47
Marin, John, 35
Marini, Marino, 200–201
Mark and Andrews Islands, 35
Martiny, Philip, 136, 221
Matisse, Henri, 106, 107, 108
Matisse, Paul, 196
McKim, Charles, 135
McKim, Mead & White, 215, 216, 218
Meadmore, Clement, 176
Medonca, George, 103
Metcalf, Willard, 115, 116
Mill at Stony Brook, 50, 53
Millbrook, 80, 94
Milles, Carl, 83
Minute Man Statue, 124
Miró, Joan, 202
Moffett, Ross, 47–48
Monet, Claude, 95, 96, 97, 115, 116, 142
Monhegan Island, 35–38
Montclair Art Museum, 6, 65, 234
Moore, Henry, 107, 173, 203, 204, 224
Moran, Thomas, 152, 153
Morland, George, 72
Morris Arboretum, 170, 171
Morris, George L. K., 126–27
Morris, Robert, 147
Morris School, 126
Morse, Samuel F. B., 148–49, 212
Motherwell, Robert, 47, 152
Mount, The, 127
Mount, William Sidney, 50–53
Murillo, Bartolome Esteban, 82
Museum of American Glass, 59

Nadelman, Elie, 107
Nagare, Masayuki, 176
Nast, Thomas, 222
Nesjar, Carl, 178
Neuberger Museum of Art SUNY, 204
Nevelson, Louise, 16, 172, 174–75, 203, 224, 226
Newhouse Gallery, 191
Newington Cropsey Foundation Gallery of Art, 109
Newport mansions, 102–4
New York Chinese Scholar's Garden, 189, 192
Noble, John, 191
Noguchi, Isamu, 170, 174, 180–83, 203, 225–26, 227
Noguchi Museum, 180–83, 185

O'Keeffe, Georgia, 12–14, 34
Olana, 8, 128–29, 130–32, 150
Old Lyme, 113–20, 147
Old Westbury Gardens, 71–73
Oldenburg, Claes, 201
Olmsted, Frederick Law, 131
Olmstead, Wes, 207
Orozco, José Clemente, 140, 231–33

Page, Russell, 199
Pamet River, 48
Panone, Joe, 207
Paolozzi, Eduardo, 175
Parrish Art Museum, 155
Parrish, Maxfield, 136
Partridge, William Ordway, 216, 217
Peace Dale, 127
Pepper, Beverly, 233
PepsiCo, Donald M. Kendall Sculpture Garden, 196–204
Peters Valley Craft Center, 61–65
Pevsner, Antoine, 177
Picasso, Pablo, 172, 178
Piccirilli, Attilio, 216, 219–20, 222
Pinto, Jody, 185
Pissarro, Camille, 95, 97
Pollock, Jackson, 151–54
Pollock-Krasner House and Study Center, 151–54
Pomodoro, Arnaldo, 147, 177, 200, 202

Poore, Henry Rankin, 115
Pope, John Russell, 215, 216, 218, 220
Price, Art, 202
Price, Bret, 203
Princeton University, 172–79
Provincetown, 45–49
Provincetown Art Association, 45, 46–47
P.S. 1 Contemporary Art Center, 186

Raeburn, Sir Henry, 72
Ranger, Henry Ward, 114, 115
Renoir, Pierre, 96
Reynolds, Joshua, 72
Rhind, John Massey, 215
Rickey, George, 170, 172, 194, 196, 201–2
Rivera, Diego, 232
Rivers, Larry, 153
Robertson, Anna Mary (Grandma Moses), 39–43
Rodin, Auguste, 201
Rogers, James Gamble, 219, 221
Rook, Edward, 115, 119
Rosenberg, Harold and May, 152
Rosenthal, Tony, 147
Rothko, Mark, 47
Rothschild, Gail, 194
Rousseau, Henri, 97
Ryder, Albert Pinkham, 143

Saar, Alison, 185
Saint-Gaudens, Augustus, xii, 123, 125, 133–40, 211, 219, 221, 234
Saint-Gaudens, Louis, 137
Salmones, Victor, 202
Sanford, Edward, 216, 218
Saret, Alan, 186
Sargent, John Singer, 18, 72, 82, 143
Sargent-Murray-Gilman-Hought House, 18
Schwartz, Buky, 170
Segal, George, 175, 201
Serra, Richard, 186
*Shaw Memorial,*138
Shay, Ed, 196
Sherk, Scott, 171
Siegel, Julie, 207
Simmons, Edward, 115
Siquireros, David Alfaro, 232
Sisley, Alfred, 115
Sloan, John, 16
Smith College, 117
Smith, David, 12, 14, 172, 178, 200, 224, 227
Smith, Tony, 178, 202
Snelson, Kenneth, 179, 201, 227
Snug Harbor, 187–92
Socrates Sculpture Park, 180, 183–86
Spencer, Niles, 47, 48
Springs, The, 153, 154
Sproat, Christopher, 195
Stachura, Joseph, 83
Stackhouse, Robert, 185
Starrucca Viaduct, 28
Staten Island Botanical Garden, 188, 190–91
Stella, Joseph, 221
Sternal, Thomas, 171
Stieglitz, Alfred, 12–13
Stone, Edward Durell, 199
Storm King Art Center, 7, 11, 109, 223–28
Storm King Mountain, 5–6, 10
Streeter, Tal, 227
Stuart, Gilbert, 104
Sugar Loaf, 65, 66–67, 86
Sugarman, George, 170
Suris, James, 207
Susquehanna Valley, 28–30
Sveinsson, Asmundur, 203

Thaxter, Celia, 32–34
Thomas Cole House, 128–30, 132, 150

Toole, Frank, 207
Toulouse-Lautrec, Henri, 82
Townley, Hugh, 196
Trumbauer, Horace, 164, 169
Trumbull, John, 22
Turrell, James, 186
Twachtman, John, 115, 120–21, 143, 144, 145

Union Church, 106, 109
Untermyer Park, 87–90, 106, 109
Upjohn, Richard, 210, 211

Vail, Lorraine, 171
van Gogh, Vincent, 95, 97, 98
Vaux, Calvin, 131
Victoria mansion, 90
Von Rydingsvard, Ursula, 227
Von Schlegel, David, 147
Vonnoh, Bessie, 115
Voorhees, Clark G., 114, 116

Watts, Peter, 82–83
Wei, Wang, 92
Weir Farm, 120, 136, 142–46
Weir, J. Alden, 5, 115, 120, 142–46
Weir, John Ferguson, 5, 143
Weir, Robert, 5, 143
Wellfleet, 44, 45
West Laurel Hill Cemetery, 159–71
West Meadow Beach, 53
West Point, 11, 132
Wethersfield, 80–83, 94
Wexler, Allan, 195, 196
Wheaton Village, 57–60
White Creek Center, 41
White, Stanford, 135, 137, 139, 211, 217
Whitney, Gertrude Vanderbilt, 217, 218
Windsor, 140–41
Wistar, Caspar, 57–58
Woodlawn Cemetery, 209, 214–22
Wren, Christopher, 213
Wright, Russel, 106, 108–9, 150
Wyeth, Jamie, 36
Wynne, David, 202, 203, 204

Young, Mahonri, 145

Zeitlen, Alexander, 221

About the Authors

Marina Harrison and Lucy D. Rosenfeld are lifelong friends and walking companions. They have collaborated on nine guidebooks, including *Gardenwalks in New England, the Mid-Atlantic States*, and *the South* (The Globe Pequot Press); *Serendipitous Outings Near New York City* (The Globe Pequot Press); *Artwalks in New York;* and *Green New Jersey*. Both enjoy discovering new places of natural beauty and historic and artistic interest.